The Vietnamization of Private Gray: Tiger Tooth

A story of a soldier's change in view of his world

By:

Gary W Gray

About the Author

Born in Walnut Ridge, Arkansas, Gary Wayne Gray has led a distinguished life of service, education, and leadership. His military career began in 1968 when he enlisted in the United States Army, where he served with dedication until 1976. Gray was stationed in Vietnam from 1969 to 1972 with Company B, 93rd Engineer Battalion. After his tour in Vietnam, he was assigned to the 63rd Ordnance Company at Fort Lewis, Washington; the 702nd Maintenance Battalion at Camp Casey, Korea; and the 43rd Engineer Battalion at Fort Benning, Georgia. He remained a U.S. Army Reservist from 1980 to 1996, 411th Engineer Battalion, Fort DeRussy, Hawaii.

Following his active duty military service, Gray completed higher education through a Bachelor of Science degree from Warner Pacific University in 1995 and a Master of Counseling degree from the University of Arkansas at Little Rock in 2003. His career in public service includes roles with the U.S. Navy Department of Transportation and various human service organizations across the U.S., from Portland, Oregon, to Jonesboro, Arkansas.

Gray further pursued his professional journey by moving his base abroad as he taught at an elementary school in MaJI, South Korea from 2005 until 2009. From 2009 to 2019, he worked as an employee of Pathfinder Inc. in Jacksonville, Arkansas,. As a multifunctional person, Gray has been enabled to dedicate his life to the cause of service education, and to help communities in his country as well as abroad.

Acknowledgments

"This book is dedicated to:

My daughter, Lisa Michell Nelson

My son, Jack Wayne Gray

All the Women that have loved me so far."

Table of Content

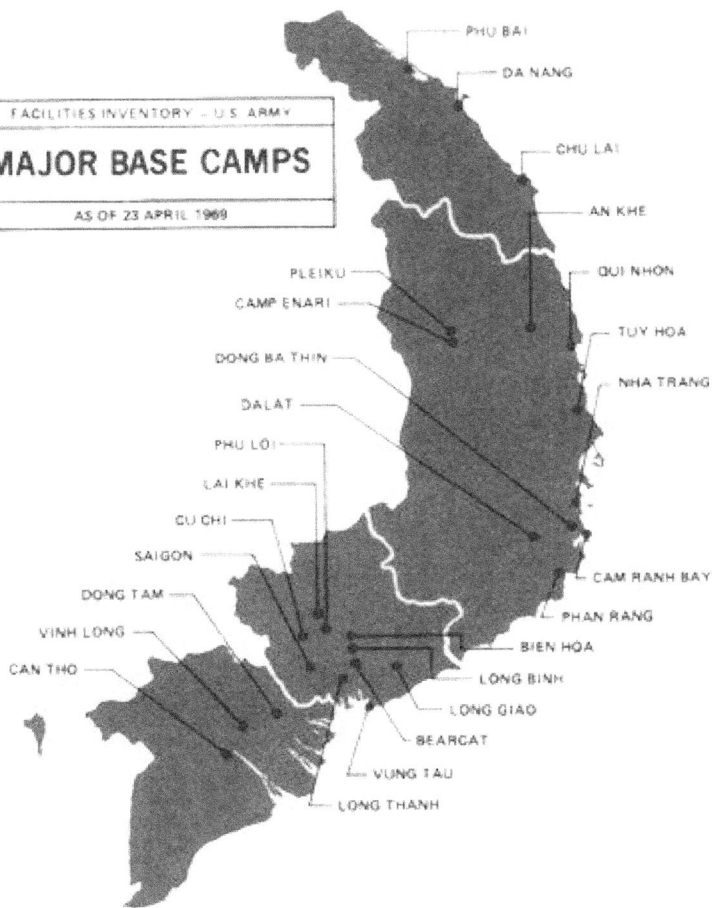

FACILITIES INVENTORY — U.S. ARMY

MAJOR BASE CAMPS

AS OF 23 APRIL 1969

PHU BAI
DA NANG
CHU LAI
AN KHE
PLEIKU
QUI NHON
CAMP ENARI
TUY HOA
DONG BA THIN
NHA TRANG
DALAT
PHU LOI
LAI KHE
CU CHI
SAIGON
DONG TAM
CAM RANH BAY
VINH LONG
PHAN RANG
CAN THO
BIEN HOA
LONG BINH
LONG GIAO
BEARCAT
VUNG TAU
LONG THANH

Chapter 1

90th Replacement Battalion May 14, 1969

T he wheels of the C-141 Starlifter screeched loudly as they hit a fumed asphalt runway on a U S Airforce base on the outskirts of Bien Hoa, South Vietnam. I watched the canvas-covered sandbagged tents flash by as the aircraft rolled down the runway.

"WELCOME TO "TAN SON NHUT AIR BASE,"

stated a sign hanging above a large aluminum hanger at the edge of the runway. I stood up and grabbed my personal carry-on items from the overhead compartment as the captain's voice came over the speaker system.

"Remain in your seats until you have been briefed by the Airforce representative," he relayed as he shut down the aircraft systems.

The flight attendants open the cabin door. The midday heat crept slowly through the aircraft, displacing the cool cabin freshness. After a few minutes, the heat from outside flooded the cabin. Sweet started to bead on my forehead and trickled down my face. I eased back on my seat, trying to relieve my cramping legs and aching back. I glanced down at my wristwatch to check the time. The time was 1400 hundred hours,

"Damn, I wished they would get this show on the road," I said under my breath.

We left Travis Airforce base 18 hours earlier. We had finally reached our destination. I had sat in the seat so long that my ass felt like it was attached to it. I glanced at the ground around the aircraft and noticed ground support personnel scurrying about preparing for our dismemberment. An Airforce Tech Sargeant dressed in a neatly pressed short-sleeved uniform appeared at the front row of the cabin. He started with,

"On the behalf of the Airforce, I welcome all of you to the Republic of Vietnam. I hope that your stay here will be a safe and pleasant one. After you disembark the aircraft, you will notice some military buses parked outside. After you have retrieved your bags, board the busses and wait for further instructions," he instructed.

He walked to the rear and opened a panel on the side of the plane. He then pulled a red handle that lowered a large rear cargo door that opened down, resting on the tarmac. It provided a ramp-like egress for us to disembark. I gathered my carry-on bags and stood waiting impatiently for my turn to get in line and march down the ramp. The line marched in a controlled manner, as is the standard military procedure for aircraft disembarkation. I stepped from under the shade of the aircraft wing onto the tarmac. A blast of hot wind stirred up by the passing of a F-14 jet and the hot blazing sun reminded me of what hell must be like. I chased after my garrison cap that was blown off my head by the blast of the jet. The cap had stopped against the legs of a short, chubby troop that was walking in front of me. He reached down, picked it up, and handed it back to me.

"God! This must be the hottest place on Earth," he said.

"I'll agree with that, it must be what it's like stepping through the gates of hell," I replied as I got in step beside him.

"I sure as hell hope that it's not this hot all over. I have an 11 Bravo MOS. I sure hope we don't have to do much walking" he said as he took out a handkerchief from his pocket and wiped his brow.

I sure felt sorry for this guy. I had volunteered to join the Army 20 days after my eighteenth Birthday. The Army recruiter had promised if I volunteered before I was drafted, I would have my pick of Military Occupation Specialty (MOS). He also promised that I would not have to go to Vietnam. He told me that I would be assigned a 62L20 MOS (Wheeled Tractor Scraper Earthmover Operator) and most likely be assigned to an engineer battalion in Germany.

The chance of being assigned in Germany was another reason I chose the Army to enlist. Hearing stories told by my boss at work about his adventures when serving in the Army while stationed in Germany. Here I was, six months later, waiting in line to go to a heavy construction engineer company somewhere smack dab in the middle of the My Cong Delta. There would be no German adventures for me.

Vapor and fumes danced around my feet, steaming up from puddles of water left over from an onslaught of a midday Monsoon rain. This would be an everyday occurrence for the next four months. I glanced around and noticed various types of aircraft concealed behind makeshift revetments. The revetments were constructed with 10-feet x 15-inch sheets of prefabricated steel planking (PSP). The metal sheets were primarily used for the construction of chopper pads and command officer parking areas. The PSP revetments were stacked in rows about four feet apart and held upright by long metal stakes with dirt filled in between. Combat Infantry Teams weighed down with TA 50 field gear were loading and unloading from the choppers; they had just returned or were going on missions.

An airport baggage caravan crossed in front of us, as we stopped to let it pass. I noticed Aluminum body size coffins strapped on top of the trailers.

"Dead Bodies," I said to the troop walking beside me. He looked at the trailers with a worried expression on his face. I could tell what he was thinking. I looked around for our luggage and noticed that there was a pile of duffle bags stacked under the wing of our aircraft. We walked over to recover the bags. I waited until the pile had dwindled before locating mine. I picked it up and slung it over my shoulder. There were a couple of buses parked at the edge of the tarmac, patiently waiting for us to load and ride to our next destination, the 90th Replacement Battalion. The replacement center was located between a couple of small hills beside the road to Saigon. The nearest city was Bien Hoa and Tan San Nhut Airbase. A few

miles towards the south was located the huge Army Headquarters of Long Binh. I climbed aboard one of the buses for the ride to the replacement center. Normally, being the loner that I am, would have walked to the back of the bus to find a seat. Instead, the strangeness of my situation, the feeling of being alone and not knowing what was going to happen next compelled me to sit in the first seat I could find. A Staff Sargeant was sitting in the seat and moved over against the window, giving me room.

"How is everything? "I asked

"Hell of a waste," he replied, nodding his head towards the crew loading coffin-like containers into the hold of the C141.

"Hell of a way to get a return trip home, "I replied.

"Sure, as shit is, I'm not going home that way," he answered.

"I'm PFC Gray," and stuck my hand out.

"Staff Sergeant Smith," he replied, grasping my hand in a strong grip.

The windows of the bus were covered with reinforced wire mesh. I was my guess that this was to prevent explosives from being thrown into the bus when the windows were down. I would have enjoyed the ride better if the windows had been up. The smell from the side of the road was overpowering. We left Tan San Nhut, wove our way through Ben Hoa, and traveled south to towards the 90th` Replacement Center. Our Convey of buses passed hastily constructed refugee camps of metal sheets with Coke stamped all over on them. It seemed to me that someone had stolen the sheets from a Coca-Cola canning factory and made small huts. Shoeless, dirty-faced kids ran along the side of the bus when it had to slow down through congested areas.

Their hands were held out, begging, "You give me candy, you give me a cigarette, you give me chop-chop."

A troop sitting in the front seat pushed a hand full of coins through the wire mesh covering the windows. The coins fell and

bounced on the asphalt, some rolling under the bus. A scream of pain rang out. I assumed that one of them had been hit when he ran under the bus to retrieve a coin. The driver didn't stop. He revved up the engine and continued down the road.

Sergeant Smith shook his head in disgust. "He should not have done that. It's one of the dangers we are warned about during orientation. If the family finds out who was driving the bus, the Vietnamese government will make the driver pay for medical treatment."

Later, during my tour, I discovered the truth of his statement. I looked around and was dismayed by the hardships and helplessness the children seemed to be enduring. After about a thirty-minute drive, we arrived at the front gates of the 90 replacement Center. The entrance was closed by two makeshift gates opened by guards to let us through. A sign above the gates read,

"90th Replacement Battalion."

As soon as we arrived, we unloaded from the buses and were assigned to barracks to wait for processing and assignments. The barracks were long buildings with concrete floors. The walls were built from 1in x 8in wood boards placed at an angle to keep rain out and allow a breeze to pass through. Army cots were placed side by side in rows on each side of the building. The next morning after chow, the troops lined up on the parade field to wait for their names to be called and unit assignments. The meetings were called shipping formations and were held each morning and after lunch. It wasn't until after the third day that my name was called. If our name was not called, we were detailed for assignments around the center and participated in in-country orientation activities. The very first thing we had to do was change all our US currency to Military Pay Certificates (MPC). We were not allowed to keep any greenbacks and had to turn in the coins we had. We were notified that it was a court martial offense to process any greenbacks.

The orientation included brushing out teeth with Silver Diamine Fluoride and listening to lectures about the dangers of drinking and eating local foods. We were also assigned TA 50 field

gear and gas masks. We did not have KP because the center had Vietnamese nationals doing the duties. This was the first time that I heard the Vietnamese language. I was fascinated and felt left out because I did not understand what they were saying. This feeling stayed with me all the time I was in Vietnam and facilitated my learning to read, write, and speak fluent Vietnamese.

I chose a cot next to the front door of the hooch. There were ten to fifteen troops already settled in. A few minutes later, Sgt White came in and flopped his luggage on the cot next to mine.

"Sarge, is this your first tour in Vietnam," I asked.

"I'm on my second tour. I just returned from vacation with my wife in Hawaii," he replied.

"What unit are you with?"I asked

"I'm in the 3rd Brigade, 9th Infantry, and my unit is stationed at Dong Tam down in the Delta. You want a smoke ? he asked, holding out a pack of Lucky Strikes.

"No thanks, I never picked up the habit yet."

"It's a good thing you said yet you'll have all kinds of habits by the time you leave this hell hole."

"Not if I can help it," I answered.

"One thing for sure, you'll be a favorite with the hooch maids. They'll hit you up to buy them cartons of cigarettes; they take them home and sell them on the black market. If I were you, I'd save them and buy a piece of ass. How old are you anyway?"

"Just turned nineteen last November. Guess I'll spend my twentieth over here," I mused.

"Nineteen? Hell, kid, you aren't old enough to have a piece of ass," he laughed.

I didn't quite agree with him. He seemed to think us nineteen and twenty-year-olds were only old enough to get killed. I sat for a while in silence, feeling hurt not wishing to carry the conversation any further. I guess Sergeant White seemed to sense my fear and frustration.

"Hell, man, I didn't mean to make you feel bad. It's just that I have met so many guys just like you who are just kids. I get to know them only to watch them die. The thing that really pisses me off is the Army keeps sending them over here."

"That's okay, Sarge, I understand," I answered.

He must have seen many men killed in action; I knew that the 9th was getting hit hard all over Vietnam.

"What's your MOS?" he asked as if reading my thoughts. "62L20, Wheeled Tractor Operator," I answered. "What's that, some kind of forklift?" he inquired.

"No, it's a huge tractor that pulls a scraper on the back to remove topsoil and level areas to be improved," I replied.

"Hey, I know what those things are. I pulled guard for the engineers when they cleared the roads around Dong Tam. You will probably get assigned to one of the engineer units stationed there," he told me.

"Isn't that kind of dangerous?"I asked.

"Not as dangerous as walking into a VC ambush," he answered. "I'm going to get some shuteye, got to head over to the chopper pads and catch a lift back to Dong Tam in the morning," he said as he lay back on the cot and was soon fast asleep.

The next morning, when I awoke. SSgt Smith and his gear were gone. I walked outside the barracks to take a look around. Troops were walking about the clean white cement sidewalks that ran between rows of prefabricated tin roof dwellings. Behind these rows of buildings were large warehouses filled with TA-50 field gear, jungle fatigues, and other supplies needed to make war. A staff Sergeant, wearing a drill instructor's hat, came out from a hooch just behind the welcoming sign. His uniform was starched stiff, and his stateside boots shined like new pennies.

"Get your asses in gear and make some kind of a formation," he bellowed.

Most of us were recruits just out of Basic and AIT; we were accustomed to responding to barking Drill Sergeants. Hurriedly, we huddled into a halfhearted formation.

"When I call for a formation, I expect a formation, not a circle jerk," he bellowed once more as he walked up and down our ranks.

"What did you say, Sargeant," he stopped in front of a well-weathered troop with Buck sergeant chevrons on his sleeves.

"I said fuck you and your formation," the Buck Sargeant answered, loud enough for everyone could hear.

"Get your ass out of my formation," the staff Sargeant retorted angrily.

"All E-4s and above fall out; turn in a copy of your orders and report to the supply room; all others standfast," he said as he turned his back to the Buck Sargeant and walked off angrily.

The Staff Sargeant disappeared back inside the operations hooch. After a few minutes, another E-6 came out; he was wearing a bonnie hat and jungle fatigues. He didn't have the ridiculous, inflated attitude that the first staff had.

"Gentlemen and troops," he addresses us. I want to take the opportunity to welcome you to Vietnam. The longest hat most that

you will stay here in Long Binh will be a couple of days. Then, you will be processed to your units. All ranks below E -4 will be put on details until your orders have been processed. The rest of you standfast. The 90th Replacement cadre will be by to assign you to different details. You will give your orders to them, and they will get them processed."

We stood around as groups of five to ten were marched off to various details; in a very short time, five others and I were all that was left of the formation.

"Looks like we got out of pulling any details,"

"I'm sure glad that Buck Sargeant put that dude Staff Sargeant straight. I was just about ready to tell him to piss off myself."Said a black soldier standing next to me."

"Yeah, the guy seemed like a complete asshole. Wonder where they got him from anyways?"

I saw a Specialist Fifth Class (SPC E-5) in cook's whites walking down the sidewalk toward us. He walked up to the remainder of us.

"So you guys are the lucky ones," he said.

The black soldier rolled his eyes and responded to the comment.

" hey man, I'll only count myself lucky if I makes it out of this hell hole alive," he retorted:

"You got a point there, soldier. All you guys secure your gear and carry it down to building 17, find yourselves a bunk, then go to supply and draw some linen if you want to. Just be down as soon as I take all your orders over to operation and start getting them processed," the cook instructed.

Building 17 wasn't too hard to find, and since all of us were spent from our plane ride, we all elected to flop down on top of the plastic-covered mattress for a short catnap instead of going to supply and checking out bedding. We all were lying on top of our bunks, waiting for the sergeant to return, when a PFC spoke up.

"Hey, you guys, I heard the SPC5 say that we were going to the 0 Club to pull K P. The last time I came through the 90th, I stuck with K P at the 0 club. They got all these gooks to do the work, Hell, the last we stayed about fifteen minutes and then split back to our hooches," commented the PFC.

The black guy looked as if he was thinking the matter over

"Right on, this nigger sure as the hell aint gonna pull no kitchen police if'n I can help it," he said.

After talking it over, the rest of them agreed with a scheme they came up with just might work, and they all were willing to give it a try.

The black guy turned to me.

"Hey you, how about it, you with us," he asked?

"Sounds good to me," I agreed halfheartedly.

"Then that's the plan," exclaimed the PFC, who had dreamed up the fool-ass plan, as he swung back around and propped his dirty boots back up on top of the bunk rail and soon was fast asleep.

The SPC5 came back still carrying his clipboard. He walked up and kicked the bunk of the PFC that had hatched up the cut-and-run scheme.

"Get your dirty ass boots off that bunk, all of you get up and get your shit together; I'm going to take you guys to the 0 club to pull KP and another thing; if any of you have any ideas about cutting out on this detail, forget it. The CO put out the word that anyone leaving a detail before they are released will be held over and pull details for an extra week."

The SPC 5 marched us off to 0 Club, which was down close to the main gate that we had come through earlier. He brought us inside and introduced us to the cooks as being the evening KP detail. We all were assigned different duties, and as usual, I got pots and pans. I walked back into the wash rack area, unwashed pots and pans were stacked up higher than my head. Well, I thought to myself. I just as well get started, or I'll be here all night. I removed my Khaki top and wadded in on them. After about two hours of sweat and elbow grease, the pile had dwindled down to almost nothing. I sat down on a stool and peered out through the screen on the porch. Darkness was already setting in. Off in the distance beyond the perimeter of the compound, lanterns flickered through the windows of thatched Bamboo huts.

The scenery was so forlorn and peaceful that it was hard to believe that so many dangers lurked out beyond the safety of the compound. A soft, gentle touch tapped me on the shoulder, disturbing me from my solitude.

"You finnie all pan already?" asked a sweet voice in broken English.

"You boo -cu workee, now you take break, all KP di-di mau, one you all stay here," She directed further.

"Yeah, I know they said earlier that they were going to cut out the first chance they got."

"You like drankee coke -ca, come inside bar and drink coke -ca, my name Mai, I bartender, you help me carry ice to bar ok," She requested.

"Sure, Mai, I'll carry the ice for you. Just show me where it is," I answered.

"Come, I'll show you. What your name?" she asked as I followed her back through the kitchen to a huge Walkin freezer.

"My name's Gary. Is the ice inside here," I asked as I opened the heavy freezer door.

"Yes, you please bring one block to the bar," she instructed as she left me and went back to the bar," she requested.

I grabbed the ice tongs and hooked them into a block of ice and lugged it into the bar. A few officers were sitting at the bar. It was only 2000 hours and most of them seemed to be already stoned out of their minds. Mai motioned me to one of the empty stools at the end of the bar. As I sat down, one of the young lieutenants eyed me suspiciously as Mai came over, leaned against the bar, and started talking to me.

"Who's that guy, your new boyfriend?" he asked her.

"No sir, I just met this young lady; I'm on K P detail," I replied before she could give him an answer.

"Just joking, soldier, whereabouts are you from back in the world?."

"Arkansas, sir," I answered.

"Like to sit here and bullshit with you, but you had better get your ass back in the kitchen. If the commander stops by and catches a private setting at the bar, he'll have all of our asses."The LT informed me.

"Hey, shithead, leave that private alone. The commander never comes in here. He's drinks with his big shot buddies over at the command headquarters in Saigon; shit, you're just jealous because Mai's paying too much attention to him," said his sidekick

After that statement, they got into a drunken argument over who was going to buy me a beer. I settled the argument by declining both of their offers and decided that I should get the hell out before they pulled me into their disagreement.

"Thanks for the Coke Mai," I told her as I got down off the barstool and went back into the kitchen. She followed me back into the kitchen.

"You good luck, sometimes you come back to Long Binh, You come talk to me." she requested.

"I sure will," I said as I got my Khaki shirt and put it back on.

"The SPC5 isn't around when he comes back; tell him that if he needs me, I'll be in building 17," I requested of her.

"No worry, Cook, no look for you. You stay longer than all GI," she replied. After I got back to building 17, I didn't see any of the group, although I did notice that their gear was still by their bunks. I didn't pay any more attention to them. The poor sleep and the K P detail left me pretty beat. I flopped out on my bunk, and in no time, I was sound asleep.

My sleep was dreamless and short. I was rudely awakened by the blinding glare of the overhead barracks lights.

"Ok, sleeping beauties out of those bunks. I got a list of names that are scheduled for a 0600 flight," someone was bellowing.

I peeped out between my squinted, sleep-filled eyes to get a glimpse of who was talking. I didn't recognize the person so I squinted at my watch to check the time, it was only 0330, no wonder it seemed as if I had only been sleeping for ten minutes. I swung my feet to the floor and started lacing my boots. I was wide awake by the time my name was called from the list.

"If I have called you from this list," a staff sergeant was saying. I focused my eyes on the person who was talking. I had seen him the day before, standing in a group of soldiers, reading names from his clipboard. He must be the transpiration coordinator. I must pay strict

attention to what he has to say. I thought to myself as I stood up and moved closer to the circle of troops gathered around him.

"As I was saying, if your name was on this list, you have only two and a half hours to draw your Fatigues and TA-50 field. All personnel must be in jungle fatigues when you board your flight," he ordered.

I gathered all my gear together and dragged it down to the area near the welcoming sign. There was a group of fifteen to twenty

men standing around waiting for transpiration. They were being briefed by the same staff sergeant who had awakened us. Again, he was calling out names, but this time, the names were from copies of orders that he was handing out to the group. He called out my name just as I walked up to the edge of the group.

"Gray, Pvt. Gary Gray," he called out.

"Here, Sargeant," I called out, walking up and holding out my hand to receive the orders as he handed them to me.

"Have you been issued your clothing and TA 50?" he asked me.

"Not yet, I haven't had time," I replied.

"Well, you had better double-time down to the supply sheds, draw your gear, and beat ass back down here if you want to leave this morning.

"Yes, Sargeant, I'll be right back," I said as I turned around and doubled timed down to the supply sheds. I hurriedly went through the line, grabbing jungle fatigues from huge stacks piled on top of homemade wooden tables. I didn't know exactly what size I wore, so I held them up in front of me. If they looked like they might match my size I took them. I grabbed a waterproof bag and started packing it with field gear. Since steel helmets and liners were first, they went in the bottom of the bag. After I had drawn the rest of my field gear, I hightailed it back to the staging area.

The rest of the group was already aboard a duce-and-half, which was waiting with it's engine running.

"Hey, troop, get your ass in gear. We're waiting on your ass," bellowed the driver while impatiently racing his engine.

As I threw my gear aboard the truck, I noticed Sargeant White sitting on the wooden slatted troop seat.

"Well, Private Gray, we met again," he said as he grabbed my hand to help me pull myself aboard.

"You must be going to the 93rd after all," he said as I sat down beside him on the troop seat.

"I don't know where I'm headed. I just climbed aboard as I was told.

"Fuck the Army and their mushroom theories," he retorted disgruntlingly.

"I just got my orders this morning and haven't had the time to look them over," I replied.

"Yeah, I know, that's the mushroom theory in operation. Keeping you in the dark and feeding you shit."

The duce-and-half launched forward, its frame giving a tired groan. It rattled out through the stone-hedged gate and rolled through a small village that lined the road just outside of Long Binh. I set back to breathe a breath of fresh air, but there was no escape from the eye-watering choking black smoke belching from the vehicle's exhaust pipe. I gave up trying to breathe and settled down to listen to a conversation between the two guys sitting next to me.

" hey man, do you know what went down last night," asked a spec four sitting to the left of me.

"No, man, what happened," inquired his partner.

"Well, it was like this: last night, while I was on CQ duty, we got a call on the radio from the 725th MPs. Seems like this black guy and three white guys sneaked off base last night to visit a whore house. They caught one of those three-wheel Lambrettas. They hit a command-detonated mine. It blew them and the pap-san, driving the Lambretta all to hell," he informed us all.

As the spec four went on to explain the details, a chill ran through my spine as the description of the four guys sounded somewhat familiar. I turned to the troop conveying the story and asked,

"Is that all the information you got on the incident?"I asked him

"The only other thing is that they arrived yesterday and that they had been assigned details at the 0 Club," he replied

"Oh my god! Those were the guys that cut out from the detail," I said aloud.

"Did you know those guys?" he asked me.

I went on to explain how all of us had been assigned KP at the 0 Club and that the four of them hatched up the plot to cut out as soon as the SPC 5 cook turned his back.

"Damn good thing you didn't join them," he said with concern.

"I would have if I hadn't been up to my elbows in pot and pans," I replied.

"Damn, the first time I ever heard pots and pans saving a life," I said.

After we had retraced our previous route from the day before, we ended up back on Tan San Nhut, very close to the same area where I had arrived the day before. The duce-and-half up close behind a camouflaged four-engine prop whose flight crew was busy making last-minute flight checks. One of the crew members told us to bring our gear and climb aboard. I walked up the belly ramp into the cargo compartment. All the seats had been removed, leaving no place for passengers to sit. What little space left was taken up by radio equipment and pallets of beer. After we all had got aboard we stood stupidly wondering what we were to do next. The co-pilot made his way from the cockpit back to where we were standing.

He leaned over and gave the cargo netting securing the radio equipment and cases of beer a hard tug. After seeming satisfied, he then turned and looked us over thoughtfully.

"Dig out your helmets and use them to sit on. Now has come the time to utilize them for what they were intended for, that is, to protect your asses. We may, and usually do, receive small-arms fire while flying over the Delta region. If we do, just sit still until we get out of get out our weapons range because there's really nothing else we can do," he instructed us.

We dug out our helmets from the bottom of our waterproof

bags, and field gear was thrown all over the cargo compartment. The resultes of everyone's helmets were on the very bottoms of the waterproof bags.

"What the Hell's wrong with those assholes at the 90th? It seems that they would know that the helmet is the last thing that should be issued every Goddamn time it's this way," the co-pilot said disgustedly as he made his way back to the cockpit.

We sat on top of our helmets while the crew chief threw a cargo strap over our stretched-out legs and secured us to the corrugated metal floor. He then secured our gear and closed the belly ramp, giving a thumbs up to the co-pilot; we were ready to embark on the next leg of our destination.

The Aircraft taxied down the runway and was up in the air before the crew had a chance to buckle themselves in the few seats that were left for them to sit. We flew south over small rivers, canals and small villages. I could see the mirror like reflection of the freshly filled rice paddies down below. Every now and then the reflection would be interrupted by the black silhouette form of a water buffalo. At times, it was being prodded by a pointed hat pajama wearing farmer or lazily grazing with a kid perched upon it's back.

After about forty-five minutes of flying time, the C-123 started descending toward the ground as if it were preparing to land. I looked down below, and the jungle was all I saw. After we were about tree top level, the pilot threw the engines in reverse, almost causing the aircraft to stall in midair. Suddenly appearing out of nowhere, was a quarter-mile strip of PSP runway. The aircraft touched down, traveled about a hundred yards, then spun around and taxied up close to an AirForce storage connex. The crew chief loosened the strap that had us snugged to the floor, then lowered the belly ramp.

"Ok, you guys, end of the ride, hurry and get your asses off this aircraft so we can get the hell out before Charily gets his motor tubs set up," he ordered.

We hurriedly grabbed our gear and exited the aircraft. In record time, the aircraft was up and away, even before we had all our gear stacked against the side of the connex. As I glanced around, I noticed the entire runway was constructed from lengths of perforated metal planking about eighteen inches wide and twelve feet long. Interlocking tongues and groves held together each length. The connex was the only other structure, except for a few aircraft revetments, on the entire runway.

I did notice that a couple of miles off in the distance was what looked like some kind of military compound. The runway. had been constructed alongside a one-lane of red dirt road that led from a small village three or four miles away to the military compound. I carried my gear on over and stacked it against the side of the connex. The sun was just beginning to peep over the top of the jungle, already, the morning air was warming up. I wiped away the few fast-forming beads of sweat from my brow and walked over to Sergeant White, "What the hell are we supposed to do now," I asked him.

"The very thing you were trained for, hurry up and wait. See that sign. It's still in the same shape as it was seven months ago; you couldn't read it then, and you can't read it now," he pointed to a faded sign hanging on the open door of the connex.

I walked around to the front of the connex to try to read the sign.

"All Incoming Personal Wishing A Ride To Dong Tam," that's all it said.

It looked like someone was going to leave a message but changed their mind, then decided to put the sign up as a joke or something.

"You know what beats the hell out of me?" asked Sergeant White as he walked up behind me.

"It is why the Vietnamese haven't stolen the damn board in the first place. Hell, I'm sure they could use it for something. Anyways, your unit is suppose to know that you are arriving this morning. There won't be anybody to pick up any of us until after 0930 hrs; vehicles aren't allowed to travel until all the roads have been cleared of mines."

The feeling of helplessness was beginning to grow by the minute as I pulled my duffel bag around into the shade behind connex. As I sat observing the close distinct of the jungle's edge, I felt more lost and helpless; the C-123 had dropped us off, leaving us weaponless and defenseless out in the middle of nowhere. I was determined to keep a close watch on the jungle lest our position be unexpectedly overran by a screaming hoard of Viet Cong. Although it was broad daylight, I could swear that ever so often, I could see melting, fleeting shadows watching us from the cover of the thick jungle vegetation.

The dirt road that lay beside the airstrip suddenly became busy with early morning traffic, which relieved some of my anxieties. Farmers harnessed to large two-wheeled carts pulled their burdensome loads to and from the glass sheet rice paddies. A young kid with a styrofoam ice chest dangling from a strap hanging from his shoulder walked up to us. He walked among us, displaying bottles of Coke packed in ice and rice husks,

"You buy coka GI? You buy coka? number one coka."Although I was becoming quite thirsty, I tried to ignore him, weighing the facts that I had been taught while in basic and AIT, among them not to buy cokes from kids. The reasoning was that the Viet Cong filled them with grind glass, which ate your stomach lining up when you drank them. We had also been instructed not to fraternize with the kids or any locals for that matter because all Vietnamese were potential enemies. Also, because of the dangers of Hepatitis, Dysentery and other exotic diseases, which they didn't even have names for as of yet, we were warned against eating or drinking of the local economy.

The sun had reached half-noon, and the heat was radiating up from the metal sheets of PSP, scorching my arms and face. My dry lips thirsted for just a drop of water, and sweat started running down my face again.

The Damn heat was inescapable. Ever so often, I would instinctively take a glimpse of the jungle. Already, I had noticed the farmers dressed in black pajamas standing in the rice fields. It was hard to tell if they were holding rifles or hoes. And there were those levees that crisscrossed each other, eventually leading to the jungle's edge. A Viet Cong could crawl down the side and be on top of us before we knew it.

As my fear and anxiety began to grow again, it was then that I noticed a movement at the jungle's edge. I blinked my eyes a couple of times to make sure that it wasn't one of the fleeting aspirations that I had been seeing. I wanted to make sure that what I was seeing was real before I announced it to everyone. I watched as what seemed like a soldier stepped from the jungle onto the rice paddy levee. When he advanced some twenty feet, another appeared behind him, and they kept coming at closer intervals until I had counted twelve. I stood up, pointing my voice filled with concern,

"Hey, you guys look over there by the jungle," I said, pointing in that direction.

Sargeant White stood up and stared at the moving troops, shielding the sun from his eyes with the flat of his hand, "Ah! It's nothing. See how big they are? There Americans; they don't grow gooks that big, probably one of the 9th LRPS." he told us.

Feeling somewhat relieved, I sat back down on my duffel bag and watched as they advanced toward us in single file. After about twenty minutes of winding around with the levees, they reach the edge of the runway. By now, they could easily be made out as Americans. They strolled across the runway toward us, hardly making a sound. From their looks, anyone could tell they were a tried and hardened lot. Most of the squad was shirtless, wearing only flak jackets and bandoliers of M-60 ammo. The belts of M-60 ammo had been distributed throughout the squad to lessen the load of the machine gunner. I also noticed that each troop carried at least three canteens of water. As they drew closer, Sargeant White exclaimed,

"Why! Those guys are from my squad," he informed us.

The squad drew around Sargeant White slapping him on the back.

"Hey, Sarge, how was Hawaii? Where's that hula girl you were supposed to bring," they all joked as happy to see him.

A tall, skinny kid sporting an M-79 grenade launcher walked up and shook hands with Sargeant White,

"Hey, Sarge, we got word that you were supposed to come in today. I'm sure the hell glad to see you; I can't control these assholes. They won't listen to a dam thing I tell them. The Viet Cong boomed the Hell out of Dong Tam last; that's why you guys had to land here. We were sent out to secure the area around Camp Viking." he informed him.

"Yeah, Serge, man," a big black carrying a M-60 machine gun spoke up, "That's why we dropped by seos. He can take you back out with us. Corporal shithead here is about to get us all killed," he informed SSgt.White

"He's right, Sarge, you know he just about called an air strike in on top of us. Here, Sarge, I brought along your scattergun," said a dark-tanned troop with a radio strapped to his back. He walked up and handed the Sarge a twelve-gauge shotgun along with a bandolier of shells.

"You crazy bastards, I'm not going anywhere until I've checked in with the first shirt. As far as I'm concerned, I'm still on R&R, until I make it back to Dong Tam."

As if on cue, a Jeep, followed by a three-quarter ton truck, came bouncing down the dirt road and skid to a stop in front of the connex. A tall, lanky lieutenant stepped down from the passenger's side and strolled up to us. Basic training reflexes caused me to spring to attention and salute. He gave me a cold stare without bothering to return the courtesy,

"What's with you shitbrain? You trying to get me killed," he said as he walked around me, walked up to Sergeant White and shook his hand.

"Sorry, Sir," I called after him.

"Sorry, don't save lives. Remember that the next time.""Yes, Sir," I replied.

"Sarge throw your gear on the back of my Jeep, and let's get the fuck out of before that crutt gets us all blown to hell," he said as he turned sharply on his heels and walked back to the Jeep.

One thing is for sure, I thought to myself as I watched the squad of troops pile on the back of the truck. I had rather get my ass chewed for saluting than for not saluting. As the convoy drove off in the direction of the military compound, the radio operator yelled out to us, "You dumb fucks, you stay out here; the V C gonna come and cut your balls off."

It got a big laugh from the rest of his compadres, but to the rest of us, it wasn't so damn funny. Soon, other vehicles began to arrive, picking up groups of two or three at a time until myself and two other guys were all that was left.

"What unit are you guys assigned to?"I asked as I got up and moved my bags closer to theirs.

"I'm going to the 93rd Engineers," replied the sandy-haired one, whose nametag read Tucker.

"Yeah, me too," replied the other.

"Then that makes three of us," I replied as I sat back down on top of my duffel bag.

"Wonder where our transpiration is," asked the third member. "Beats the hell out of me. Maybe they didn't get word that we were arriving," I replied.

The troop's nametag said his name was Mahoney; he looked like one, too, red hair and freckles covering his already badly sunburned face. The fatigues that he had been issued were much too big for his size. They made him look like a boy scout, sitting there in his bright new green boonie hat. He pulled out an OD army-issued handkerchief and wiped the sweat from his face,

"It's so god darn hot, and I'm dying from thirst," he said as he folded the handkerchief up neatly and stuck it back in his pocket.

"I agree with you. It's already past twelve hundred hours, and I'm about ready to go look for some food."I replied.

I had noticed that the kid selling Cokes had moved to the other side of the road a few yards away. He and this old mama-san were squatting on their hunches in the shade underneath her vendor's cart. I also had noticed that from time to time, people stopped buying something from her. My thirst and curiosity overcame my better judgment as I got up and walked over to where they were sitting. The old lady gave me an ugly black tooth grin and said something in Vietnamese that I didn't understand.

"How much are your cokes," I asked the kid.

"You give a me fifty dong, and I give you one coka," he replied.

"I don't have Dong, only M P C,"(Military Payment Currency, used instead of greenbacks), I replied.

"Ok, you give me one dollar MPC, I give you three coka," he told me, drawing a can of coke from the ice chest.

It didn't sound like too bad of a bargain, anyway. I was too thirsty to argue, so I gave him the money and took the cokes. Again, the old lady said something to me in Vietnamese while she pulled back a cheesecloth covering, displaying an assortment of breads, meats and vegetables.

"What's this," I asked the kid as I leaned over and took a sniff of the meat.

"Mama-san, she sells Vietnamese sandwiches, you like," he asked.

"How much," I asked, not really concerned with the price.

If I was hungry enough to eat that, I wasn't really too much worried about the price, I though to myself as I took out another MPC note and handed it to her.

"Ok, Mama-san, I'll take one of those sandwiches," I said, handing her the money and pointing to the loaves of French bread on the cart.

She gave me another ugly grin, split the loaf down the middle with a dirty-looking knife and started heaping vegetables and meat on top. After she had finished making the sandwich, she wrapped it up in a sheet of typing that had english printing on it. I thanked them both, took my sandwich and cokes, went back over to the connex, sat down and commenced to devour it.

Tucker was eyeing the sandwich with utter disgust,

"You had better not eat that. It might make you sick or even kill you," he told me.

Well, the way I see it, the Vietnamese have been eating this stiff for a hell of a long time, and I still see plenty of them walking around," I replied.

"Yeah, I guess you are right, but I don't think I can stomach one of the sandwiches. Hell, I"m going to go get me one of those cokes. I'm so damn thirsty I could drink spit. How much did they cost," he asked.

"Here, you guys can have these two cokes," I said as I handed over the cokes to them. They both tilted them up and drained the bottles until they were empty. I glanced at the print on the sandwich wrapping. It was a copy of someone's DEROS orders. I handed the sheet of paper over to Tucker,

"Take a look at this. It's a copy of someone's orders," I informed him.

He studied the orders carefully, "Well, I'll be damned, wonder where the old lady came up with them.

"You think she's VC? "I asked.

"I don't know about that but I don't think the VC would give them back to an American wrapped up with a sandwich. Damn! Man, I still don't see how you can eat that sandwich." he answered.

"I haven't eaten since I got off the plane yesterday. I am so hungry I could eat almost anything. Anyway, you guys should try one; it tastes pretty dam good," I answered.

"Ain't no telling what you're eating. We were told in basic that the Vietnamese would cook up anything that moves and eat it," Mahoney cut in.

Mahoney had also walked over to the vendor's cart and bought three more Cokes. He brought them back over and handed us each one.

"What the hell are we going to do if no one comes after us before it gets dark? I'm sure ain't going to stay out here after dark?" Tucker inquired.

"You know I've been sitting here watching, every so often, I've noticed one of those three-wheeled Lambrettas pass by. I'm thinking about trying to hire one to take us down to that military compound. What do you two guys think about that ideal?" I asked.

"Sounds good," They answered in unison.

"Good idea, we got to do something," Tucker replied.

"Ok, it's settled. We'll stop the next one that comes by," I agreed.

I waited about twenty minutes, and then I saw a Lambretta coming from the village toward our location.

Mahoney jumped to his feet, " here comes one. Hurry up, go out on the road and stop him." he said to me.

I ran out and stood in the middle of the road and started waving my arms up and down. The vehicle pulled to a stop just inches in front of me. The driver was sitting in a seat just over the front wheel. The vehicle was sort of a V-box-shaped cart with two wheels in the rear and one wheel in the front. The vehicle looks somewhat like a three-wheel motorcycle with a covered bed. A young Vietnamese lady wearing wispy silk pajama trousers under a long-sleeved high-necked split-to-the-hip dress was sitting in the rear. Trying to be as polite as possible, I said to the driver,

"Excuse me, sir, but we need some help. We would pay you if you would take the three of us and our baggage down to that military compound," I requested.

The man just looked at me, showing no expression of comprehension at all.

"Damn, I said under my breath" as the young lady said something to the driver in Vietnamese, "I got to do something about this language barrier. A big smile crossed the driver's face. He looked at me and vigorously shook his head, yes, then turned back to the young lady and said something to her in Vietnamese.

"Papa-san say yes, he takes you to compound, you each give him one one dollar MPC," she informed me.

"Hey, you guys, bring your gear over," I called out to them as I walked back to the connex.

We lugged our gear over and threw it into the back of the Lambretta. After all our gear was aboard, there wasn't any room for us to sit. The three of us clung to the side of the overloaded vehicle as it chugged down the dirt road toward the entrance to the base. The driver pulled up in front of a guard rail that blocked the road. An American soldier, standing in the doorway of a small guard shack, walked over to the weighted end of the rail. He pushed down on a huge cement block that was attached to the rail. The rail then was attached to a fulcrum mount, which allowed the end blocking the road to swing straight up to allow traffic to pass.

"Where are you guys headed?" asked the soldier as we started unloading our bags from the back of the Lambretta.

"We're on our way to Dong Tam, we've been waiting for a ride since early this morning, but no transportation showed up. We came down here to see if there were some way we could get in touch with the 93rd," I replied.

"Yeah, that happens all the time," he said with a laugh.

"I saw you guys sitting beside the connex. I was just wondering how long it would take you guys to decide to come here to look for a ride. Leave your gear here and go down to operations. They'll radio your company to come and pick you guys up," he said to us.

The young lady was walking down the road toward the center of the compound. She had walked about one hundred yards when the gate guard called out to her, "Hey Mia, come back here for a minute. I want you to show these guys where the operations hooch is," he requested of her.

She retraced her tracks back to where we were standing, "Ok, I show. Come follow me," she directed.

We followed her down the dirt road, watching the gentle sway of her hips as she stepped gracefully over potholes in the middle of the road. She reminded me of a high school tease as she glanced over her shoulder at us and gave us a flirting grin. She stopped and waited for us to catch up with her, "You live at Camp Viking?" she asked me.

"No, all of us just got here today. We are to be assigned to the 93rd Engineers at Deng Tam."

"Oh, you Cong Binh, Cong Binh number one, you make good road for Vietnam. I know Cong Bing 93, My good friend she work at 93 Castle Club. Her name Thanh. There operation hooch," she said, pointing to a building with a tin roof and wood sides.

"Thanks, Mai, for helping us. I tell Thanh you said hello," I called out after her as she walked off toward the camp club.

A shirtless, hatless soldier leaning against the sandbags stacked up in front of the hooch greeted us, "What can I do for you fellows?" he asked us with a Texas drawl.

"We need to get a hold of our unit and tell them to send us some us transportation," I replied.

"Well, you sure came to the right place, seeing as I'm the radio operator. Come and follow me."

"Hey Gray, me and Mahoney are going to the club to get us all something to drank. After you call the 93rd, come and join us," Tucker said.

"Ok, you guys go ahead. I'll be there as soon as I get through.

I followed the radio operator through the operations hooch; there were a couple of clerks busy over typewriters. I looked around but didn't see any radio equipment.

"We got to go out to the commo bunker. It's just right outside," the radio man said as he opened the screen door at the rear of the hooch.

I follow him outside to a sandbagged bunker complex. The bunker had been constructed by facing two connex toward each other and stacking sandbags around and over the top.

"Hell man, these sandbags must be six feet thick, "I exclaimed with amazement.

"You got that shit right. That's what I've been doing for the last ten months. It even took a direct hit. All I had to do was come back out and restack the sandbags. I even sleep inside there. Come on in, and I'll make the call for you."

As I entered the bunker complex, I was once again astonished. There were black lamps all over the place, reflecting screaming demons and fiery flames reaching out to me from the black velvet cloth draped at the side of the connex. The radioman gave me a chilling laugh,

"Welcome to Hades," he said.

"It's hot as hell in here, so I designed the decor to match the temperature. After you smoke a couple of joints and strip down naked, it an't too bad."

After a few tries, he got through to the 93rd. I heard a voice on the speaker box, "What do you mean no one has gone to pick those guys up? I hope the Sargeant major doesn't get word of it. He'll have somebody's ass. Tell those guys that we'll send a duce right out," the voice said.

"Guys, you heard that. They'll send someone right out to pick you up."

"Thanks a lot. I had better get over to the club and round those other guys up."

"No need to hurry. You still have plenty of time. It will take at least one hour before your transportation arrives."

"Thanks again. If you will walk over to the club with me I'll buy a beer."

"Sounds tempting, but I had better stick close to the radio," he replied.

Camp's small club. As soon as I opened the door, the clean, crisp, air-conditioned comfort surrounded me. God, how good it feels to get out of this god-forsaken heat, I thought as I walked over to where Mahoney and Tucker were leaning against the bar.

"Hey guys, our ride's on its way," I told them, just as one of the troops reached up and vigorously rang a brass ship's bell that was hanging over the bar.

"You have sure done it now, "Tucker said with a laugh. "Done what?"I asked.

"Read that sign right behind the bell," he replied. In big, bold letters, the sign read,

HE WHO ENTERS COVERED HERE BUYS THE CLUB A ROUND OF CHEER

"Oh shit," I exclaimed as I hurriedly snatched off my boonie hat from the top of my head.

"Too late now, the same thing happened to us. Both of us had to buy rounds," Tucker told me with a good-natured laugh.

I walked on over to the bar and, pulled out a ten-dollar MPC note and handed it over to Mai. "Set'um up, but give me a Coke. I need something to cut the dirt from my throat."I requested.

She laughed, "You luck, now not many man in club, all man go Chow Hall eat Chop-Chop. Only cost you one dollar twenty cents, I give you coka free."

I opened the coke up and drained the bottle, just remembering that I hadn't tasted any of the water as of yet. I turned to the troop who had rang the Bell and asked him how the water tasted.

"Hell, I don't know. I haven't drunk any in the seven months that I have been here. The only thing that I know is fit to drink is Coke and beer Unless it's Black Label. No one drinks Black Label because it tastes like warm piss." he informed me.

I turned to Mahoney and Tucker, "we had better get our asses in gear. Our ride is on it's way to pick us up."

We all left the Club together and walked back to the operations hooch to wait for our ride. I glanced once more at my watch; it was already seventeen-thirty hours, and I was dog-tired. How good it would feel to take a shower and wash off four days of filth. I saw a duce-and-half bouncing down the road coming in our direction. Soon, it was close enough that I could read it's bumper markings. 20BG 34GP 9RD HQ61, was printed in bold white letters. It bounced to a stop in front of us.

The driver leaned his head out the open window, "you, the guys that are going to Dong Tan," he asked.

"Yeah, that's where we are supposed to be heading. We've been waiting for a ride since early this morning," I replied.

"Yeah, I know, it happens all the time. The Battalion didn't get word that you guys were coming. Usually, all incoming personnel arrive at the Airfield at Dong Tam. Last night, we were under a

mortar attack. Charily boomed the hell out of the Airstrip, leaving it impossible to land planes. At least you guys had the presence of mind to come on to Viking and get a ride. Last week some newbees belonging to the 9th stayed all night out on that Airstrip. During the night, the ARVINs had a firefight on the other end of the Airstrip. It scared the Holy Hell out of them. They hightailed it down to Camp Viking, and they just about got their asses shot off as they tried to storm the gate. You guys throw your gear aboard to get back beat before it gets dark. We sure as hell don't won't to get caught outside Dong Tam after dark. This entire is infested with VC."

We threw our gear on the back of the Duce-and-half, and I noticed that the driver and his shotgun rider had their flak jackets and steel pots on. I had been issued the same things with my TA-50 gear. I dug the articles out and put them on. The shotgun rider stuck his head out the rear window canvas flap.

"I would advise you guys to do the same thing. We get sniper fire all the time, and they could save your asses. Especially when it's this close to dark, he yelled out over the noise of the engine.

I slid from the troop seat onto the bed of the truck. To Hell with being out in the open like a sitting duck, I thought. Tucker and Mahoney must have thought it was a good idea because they did likewise.

The afternoon monsoon rain raced across the rice paddies, trying to intercept us before we reached the shelter of overhanging Banyaan tree branches that shaded the jungle road. At it's entrance, peddlers huddled together, wrapped in plastic sheets, bracing themselves against the coming onslaught. The vehicle's horn blared warningly, trying to move the inadvertent peddlers to the side of the road. The horn seemed to have no effect.

They remained glued to their spots, letting the vehicle spray them with muddy water churned up from the fast-forming puddles under the vehicle's wheels. The horn blaring gear screaming engine racing the duce-and-half sent bicycles, Motorcycles and Lambrettas scurrying to the roadside, out of harm's way.

We passed a group of students returning home from school. The boys dressed in black turned-up button-down collared uniforms escorted the young ladies in virgin white silk Ao Dias, the national dress of women and young ladies. As we passed the group of students, the vehicle's wheels hi more puddles, spraying muddy water everywhere. The soiled young maidens were left standing in the middle of the mud puddle, arms hanging in limp, covered with wet, disgusting mud. The rain stopped as suddenly as it came, leaving a cool evening wind blowing through the Banyan trees. We passed through two different roadblocks that were manned by Vietnamese troops. As we approached the barbwire barriers, the soldiers would pull them aside to let us pass through.

"What the Hell are those roadblocks for?"I asked the driver as we slowed down to pass through one.

"Those guys are PF troops, something like our reservists; they man the roadblocks at night and then go back to their regular jobs during the day. The Vietnamese Government uses them to check for civilians traveling at night without ID cards. They catch a lot of Viet Cong that way." he answered.

The sun had already disappeared by the time we pulled up to the front gate of Dong Tam. The gate guards were really pissed off because they had to come out and remove the roadblocks to let us drive through. They informed us that extra security precautions had been enforced as they walked around the vehicle checking the undercarriage.

"What are you guys looking for?"I asked one of the guards who was holding a truck mirror attached to the end of a pole.

"Explosives, the Viet Gong have been sticking explosives to the undercarriages of vehicles, their heat sensory by using a weather Thermometer for a detonator."

All three of us breathed a sigh of relief as we finally were cleared to pass through the gate. We were quite glad to have finally reached our destination.

****

Chapter 2

The waters of the mighty Mekong flow down from the majestic mountains of Tibet. It's swift, muddy current snakes it's way through Laos, Cambodia, and Vietnam. Near Phnom Penh, it branches into two major tributaries. Each of these tributaries flows through rich, fertile rice land until it empties into the ocean in Vietnam's Mekong Delta region. In the Monsoon season, these waters back up, creating nature's own irrigation system through all of Southeast Asia.

Dong Tam, the home base for the 9th Infantry Division, was constructed in a rice paddy alongside one of these tributaries. Dong Tam was the largest American cantonment in the Mekong Delta; Easy excess by water made it an ideal base camp for Construction Engineering companies. Massive efforts were underway to help Vietnam become stable economically; to do the vast rice lands in the Mekong Delta were of the utmost importance. To get this valuable product to market, roads and bridges had to be built. In the early 1950s, the French had built a two-lane gravel road, that ran from Saigon through the heartland of the Delta on into. Cambodia. This was the major transportation route used to take the rich rice crops to market. Sections of this route had badly deteriorated, and long stretches were utterly impassable.

The Army Corps of Engineers submitted an eight-year proposal to reconstruct this vital roadway. RMJ-BRK, a civilian construction firm, won the contract bid to widen and pave the route, which would turn it into a major four-lane Highway. This project of connecting a vast network of oxcart roads, small rivers, and canals to the major route took nearly eight years.

The 93rd Engineers, a heavy construction Battalion belonging to the 20th Engineer Brigade, were tasked to reconstruct the Ox cart roads and build bridges. The 93rd consists of five companies: Headquarters, Alpha, Bravo, Charily, and Delta.

Headquarters, HQ as it was so affectionately known, very seldom ventured far from base camp. It's personnel mainly consisted of administrative clerks, civil engineers, surveyors, and supply personnel. HQ company was tasked to reassign all new incoming personnel to the different line companies.

Alpha company was a direct support company, meaning that they supplied mechanics and parts to keep the heavy construction equipment operational. Bravo, Charly, and Delta were line companies. They were the workhorses of the Battalion. These companies set up camps as close to job sites as possible. Many times, it was an unoccupied Vietnamese army base or some deserted French Villa. Advantages, such as Medical, PX, and Clubs, were very seldom experienced by these line companies.

The duce-and-half pulled to a stop in front of a large Engineer castle emblem sign,

"HEADQUARTERS COMPANY 93RD ENGINEER

BATTALION"

was printed in big red letters against a white background.

"End of the ride," the driver called to us.

"Where do we go from here?" I asked the driver as we climbed in the back and started tossing our bags to the ground.

"Hell, I don't know. You guys hurry and help me get these bags off. I got to take this vehicle back to the Motor Pool before the Motor

Sergeant gets pissed and makes me stay and fix flat Dump Truck tires. That building there is Ops, usually the Staff Duty NCO is in there," he pointed toward a building just behind the sign.

"Damn! I'll be glad when we can stop dragging all these bags around," Mahoney exclaimed as we all dragged the bags over to the operations hooch. We went inside and looked around,

"Wonder where everyone is?" asked Tucker,

"I don't know, but I'll stay here and wait. If you guys want, go find some chow," I replied.

"How about you? You want us to try to get you some too?" asked Tucker.

"No thanks, my stomach feels a little woozy. I think it is because of that sandwich I bought from that vending cart".

They had been gone for about twenty minutes before the Staff Duty Sargeant came back.

"Where's the other two guys?" he asked me.

"They went to try to find some chow," I replied.

"They're Shit out of luck, and the Mess Hall has already closed. You guys won't be able to do any in-processing until tomorrow morning. Go to the back row of hooches and find yourself an empty bunk. I'll tell the others when they get back," he instructed

I got all my gear together once more and set out to find the back row of hooches. I located the row of empty hooches, and they were situated beside an artillery battery. Damn, I'm sure not going to get any sleep tonight if they start firing those big guns, I thought as I stepped inside and looked around. There were about six bunks in the hooch, One of them was already occupied by a sleeping troop. I took the first empty bunk and flopped down on top. I was so tired that I didn't bother removing my boots or uniform; in no time, I was sound asleep.

Suddenly, I was startled from my sleep by an earth-shaking explosion. I set up, still half asleep, and swung my boots to the

wooden floor. The floor and walls were still shaking as I set confused on the edge of the bunk.

"What the Hell was that?"I called out through the pitch darkness. I got no answer, So I called out again," Tucker, Mahoney, you guys awake"?

As if answering my question, a brilliant orange flash lit up the open doorway. A loud vibrating boom again shocked the hooch.

"Incoming, incoming, cried a troop running down the wooden Two-by-four sidewalk that ran in front of the row of hooches.

Another brilliant flash again lit up the night sky, silhouetting the soldier as he ran past the open doorway. Bedding and mosquito netting were still clinging to him, as he had been in such haste he had forgotten them. The fourth flash sounded as if it hit really close. I didn't know if the building was shaking or if it was me trembling in my boots. I was so confused that I didn't know whether to dive under the bunk or run outside. Before I had come to a decision, someone with a flashlight came running through the hooch. He shined the flash in my direction. Seeing me still sitting on my bunk, he yelled out at me.

"You had better get the hell up and get to the bunker; Charily's walking them in on us," he said as he stopped and kicked the other guy's bunk.

"Wake this guy up and help him to the bunker, looks like he's passed out and probably been smoking dope. I'm going to check the next hooch".

I jumped up and ran over to the sleeping troop. Before I could reach him, I was knocked to the floor by another blast. I felt a sharp stinging on my right forearm and touched it, and my arm was bleeding as I crawled across the floor to the guy sleeping in the bunk.

"Hey man, wake up; we got to get to a bunker," I yelled as I grabbed hold of his arm and pulled him into a sitting position. I let go, and he fell back as limp as a dish rag. It was then that I remembered

that I didn't even know where the bunkers were; this made me more determined to awaken him. If I can just wake this guy up, maybe he can show me where the bunker is, I thought as I laid my hand on his chest to shake him harder. I shook him real hard, at the same time calling out to him, but still I got no response. I drew my hand back, feeling something sticky on my fingertips.

"What the Hell! This guy's bleeding!"I exclaimed out loud.

The guy with the flashlight ran back inside the hooch.

"Is everyone ok?" he asked.

"That round hit right outside".

"I'm fine, but I think there's something wrong with that guy over here. He wouldn't respond when I tried to wake him up," I replied.

The guy came over and shined the flashlight on the guy lying in the bunk. The beam fell on the death mask face, then traveled down the length of the body, then came back to rest on the chest area. The white tee shirt soaked blood red right over the heart.

"I'll go get the medic, but I just know it's too late. Are you sure you're ok?" he asked as he shined the flashlight back on my arm.

"Yes, I'll be all right. It's stopped bleeding," I replied.

"I haven't seen you around. What company are you in?" he asked.

"I haven't been assigned to a company as of yet. I just got into the country two days ago. I'm in the 93rd Engineers," I answered.

"93RD! Hell, man, why did they send you down here? This area belongs to the artillery?" he questioned.

I explained to him that I though I was following directions when I had picked this hooch to bed down in.

"You sure fucked up, it's a wonder that you didn't get your ass blown away. No one ever sleeps in these hoochs because there too close to the artillery pieces. Hey man! Look at your arm. It's bleeding. A piece of shrapnel must have hit you," he said with concern.

I held my arm out under the flashlight beam. I noticed a slightly bleeding cut on my upper forearm. It has just about stopped bleeding. "Looks like it was only a scratch," I replied.

"I'm going to find the Medic. I'll be right back," he informed me, then turned on his heels and disappeared through the open doorway, once again into the pitch darkness.

By now, the explosions and flashes had stopped, and a still. quietness fell over the hooch and the surrounding area. Standing beside the dead soldier was making me very uncomfortable,

"Damn, I think I'll go outside," I said aloud to no one in particular.

I stepped through the open doorway, trying to shake off the cold chills that were running up and down my spine. A blanket of pitch darkness still covered the night sky. Along the edge of the perimeter, I could see the shadowy guard towers looming against the background. Every now and then, a flare would burst high overhead, lighting up the area beyond the perimeter. Tracers from M-60 machine guns chased each other across the cleared area and disappeared into the dark outline of the jungle.

A couple of cobra gunships appeared from out of nowhere. Loud hooting and cheering broke out from troops standing along the boardwalk as the gunships belched out tongues of deadly machine gun fire at a spot on the edge of the jungle. A flashlight advancing down the boardwalk toward me caught off the jungle. A beam from a flashlight caught my attention as it advanced down the boardwalk towards me. After it had got close enough for me to hear, I recognized the voice of the troop who had gone after the medic.

"Here it is. It's this last hooch," he said to a shadowy figure walking beside him. As they drew up close to me, I noticed the other fellow carrying a medical bag.

"You the guy with the arm wound?" he asked me.

"Yeah, It's just a scratch. There's a guy inside that's in bad shape. You'd better go in and check him out first," I informed him.

We followed the medic inside the hooch.

"Shine the light on him while I check him out," he told the guy holding the flash lite.

The flashlight beam fell on the dead man's face then, traveled the length of the body, and then came back to rest on the chest area.

"You're right. He got it right through the heart," he told us as he kneeled beside the bunk, holding the dead man's limp wrist between his thumb and finger. He let go of the arm and covered the body up with a sheet that had fallen to the floor.

"Let me see the light. I'm going to check out this guy's arm," he told the guy holding the light.

The other troop handed him the flash lite, which he shined on the wound on my forearm. After poking around in the wound with a cotton swab, he informed me that there was a piece of shrapnel inside and that I should go to the dispensary first thing in the morning and get it dug out.

"Fine with me, but could one of you guys tell me how to get back to the 93rd's area?" I requested.

"Yeah, go four blocks toward the center of the compound. It's the row of hooches next to the street".

I got all my gear together and once again set out in the night to try to locate the 93rd's area. As I stumbled along in the darkness, all of the day's events came rushing at me.

Life seemed so unfair; I remembered how they had brought one of my childhood friends home. It was the first time that I had heard about it. Vietnam. I was only sixteen at the time; I remembered the funeral and how hard it had been on Mrs. Parker. I wasn't afraid of dying. It was that I just didn't want my mother to have to go through

that much grief. I prayed a silent prayer as I looked for a hooch to bed down in. God just let me make it back home in one piece.

To Hell with trying to find a bunk this time of night, I told myself. I carried my gear back up to the operations hooch and threw it down against the front of the building. Still tired from my journey, I laid my head against my duffel bag and went back to sleep.

The brilliant glare of the morning sun awoke me from a deep, dreamless sleep. The few minutes that it took to clear my head paid off. Damn, it's good to be alive, I thought as I stood up and drew in a deep breath of fresh air.

"Good God! It's almost 0900," I said aloud to no one in particular.

Trying to compose myself by straightening my uniform, I stepped inside the operations hooch. A spec 4 was sitting at a makeshift field desk. I walked up to him and introduced myself,

"I'm PVT Gray," I announced as I handed him my 201-file packet.

"I'm supposed to be assigned to the 93rd," I went on to explain.

"Well, trooper Gray, you're no longer a Private. You made PFC as soon as you came into the country," he replied as he opened my 201-file packet. He thumbed through the packet, reviewing it's contents.

"Looks like you're a heavy equipment operator. More than likely, you'll be assigned to one of the Line Companies. Where's the other two guys that came in with you," he asked.

"I have no idea. We got separated last night."I then went on to explain the sequences of events that had taken place during the night.

"Sorry about the mix-up. I'll show you where you will be bedding down for the next couple of weeks. The three of you will have to attend a two-week Survival course before the three of you go to your units," he informed us.

I followed him back outside and gathered my gear together. I sure was glad that I had only brought a duffle bag containing only my basic clothing issue. Even with that, the duffle bag and the TA-50 gear were still quite a burden to lug around. We walked down the wooden slat board sidewalk to hooch a couple of rows behind the operations hooch. Mahoney and Tucker were still sacked out on bunks. I noticed that they had also located bedding and Mosquito netting sometime during the night.

"This is the transit hooch; find yourself an empty bunk. It looks like those two guys have already located the supply room. Wake them up and get them to show you where it is. All of you come back down to see me after you get settled in, say around 1430 hours. That'll give you guys time to go and check out the PX. Oh! by the way, stop by, and I'll give you guys the paperwork to take to finance to be paid. Also, you can pick up your ration cards at the same time". He instructed.

"Thanks a lot, but the first thing I need is a shower," I called out after him as he turned to leave.

I dumped the contents of my duffle bag out on top of the bunk I had chosen. I pulled off my clothes, and just as I was wrapping an OD-colored towel around me, I heard some girlish giggles. Turning around, I saw three Vietnamese women sitting on the floor at the rear of the hooch. I hadn't noticed them when I had first came in. It was my guess that they had been setting polishing boots all the while. The women watching me in my undressed state caused me to display an amount of modesty. Quickly, I hunched down between the bunks, trying to cover myself with the towel that was much too short. This brought another flood of giggles from my audience. A middle-aged woman, who seemed to be the ring leader of the bunch, gave me a gold tooth grin.

"No sweat, GI, GI got big coom cock, Mama-san like. GI like to go Boom-Boom."

I had no idea as to what she was talking about. Later on, I discovered the meaning, I think it cost me five dollars. After I had showered and changed into a clean uniform, I decided to walk back over to the artillery unit's area and survey the damage caused by the motor attack. When I reached the hooch, I walked around to the side. The round had left a large crater, about twelve feet wide.

Sandbags that had been stacked waist-high around the side of the hooch were ripped apart, leaving fragments of shrapnel embedded in the wooden louvers. Damn, I thought, as I stood there looking at the damage, a piece of shrapnel must have flown in between the louvers, hitting the guy in the chest. It was then that I realized that just a few more feet closer, I wouldn't have been standing there looking at the damage.

I left the area ill at ease. Is this the way it was going to be? I asked myself. How discouraging it was not knowing what my chances were. I walked down to the dispensary to have the piece of shrapnel dug out and the wound cleaned. About thirty minutes later, after my arm had been cleaned and bandaged, I made my way down to the mess hall. As I was setting down to eat, the Spec. 4 clerk stopped by my table and informed me that the three of us would be leaving bright and early the next morning.

"See if you can locate those other two guys, then all of you come by my office and pick up your paperwork to get paid. This will be the last until you guys get through with the jungle training courses," he informed me.

I met Tucker and Mahoney on their way to the Chow Hall.

" hey Gray, what happened to you last night," Mahoney asked me as I stopped to give them the information I had learned.

"I spent the night dogging Motor rounds," I answered.

"Yeah, that really was something. One of the old timers we met last night while in the bunker told us that we get hit at least four or five times a week. They sure scared the holy hell out of me. I didn't know what to do. Lucky thing for us, the bunker was right next to our hooch," he replied.

"I wasn't quite as lucky. I got screwed up in my directions and ended up in the artillery's area. Charlie's been hitting the hell out of them lately, and last night was no exception. All four rounds hit in their area," I replied as I filled them in on what had happened during the night.

"Damn! Some of the people have all the luck, first day in the country, and they get a Purple Heart".

Right away, I let him know that the only thing that I considered lucky was that I was still alive".

"Hey, you guys, the company clerk told me that we were leaving for Jungle training the first thing in the morning and that we have to get all our in-processing completed this afternoon," I informed them.

The next morning came much too early; Mahoney and Tucker had kept me nearly all night with their partying. They had gotten some dope from someone. It finally put them asleep around 0200. If not, they probably would have kept me up all night. There was no morning reveille. Everyone seemed awake on their own and usually were about their jobs by 0700 hours. The company clerk came by to make sure that the three of us were up and about.

"You guys get up. Shit, shower, and shave. Meet me down at operations as soon as you eat breakfast. Since you are the only one awake, I'll leave it to you to get those other two guys up," he informed me.

At 0700 sharp, we three newbies were standing in front of the operation hooch, ready to go. We had been told to bring only our TA-50, which consisted of Ammo pouches of seven magazines each, gas mask, helmet, and flak jackets. We all looked ready for combat as we stood around, waiting for our transpiration to arrive. The only thing wrong with the pitcher was that none of us had a weapon or ammo, which caught the Sergeant Major's. Attention when he came by to give us the once over.

"Where are your weapons, soldiers?" he asked as he walked up to us and eyed us up and down.

"We haven't been issued weapons as of yet," Mahoney answered in reply.

"You guys had better high tail it down to the Armory and have some issued to you. Make sure that you are issued live ammo. I had some troops blown away a couple of months ago because they were issued blanks and then sent out to practice setting up ambushes. Charlie walked right into them, and they opened up on the V C with blanks. All the time, they thought it was a game," he informed us.

We hurried to the Arms Room, where we were issued M-16s and Bandoliers of live ammo. We took the Sergeant Major's advice and checked our ammo over carefully. When we returned to the operations hooch, the same Duce-and-half that had transported us the day before was waiting for us.

The 9th Infantry was assigned the task of securing the Mekong Delta region. As the number of casualties grew, Commanders deemed that they should establish an in-country training survival courses. These courses were extended to all other groups participating in defending the Delta region. The courses consist of "Methods of Jungle Movement,"

"Search and Destroy' "Ambushing and Counterambushing". The last three days were completed with a water survival course. Our main concern was the water survival course. Although the other courses were beneficial, they didn't pertain to our job. The first phases of training were much like those crammed into a

Two-week RVN Orientation that I had attended at Fort Benning, Georgia; just before I arrived in the country.

To connect the vast network of rivers, streams, and canals to the main transportation route, the engineers had to construct many bridges. This being the case, the "Water Survival Course was our main concern.

On the third day of the last week, all of us were loaded onto the rear of Duce-and-halfs and transported to Camp Viking. This is where the Water Course had been set up. Camp Viking had been built by a Reserve Unit that had been deployed in the mid-sixties. They had chosen one of the small canal tributaries that flowed into the My Kong, a short distance East of My Tho city. The spot that had been chosen for the water survival course was a small canal that flowed into the river. The front gate of Camp Viking, being only a couple hundred yards away, made the area essentially secure.

Since Mahoney, Tucker, and I were the only engineers in the group, we steadfastly became a team. The first morning, we were instructed on techniques of navigating and crossing waterways. Using Infantry squad movement tactics, we would walk down a small path, cross the canal, turn around, and repeat the tactical movement. The object was to keep our weapons and ammunition dry. After about the fourth trip to the top of the Red clay bank, the surface was so slippery that we had to ram our rifle muzzles into the mud in order to negotiate the course. Around lunchtime, the primary instructor called us all together and told us to knock off for lunch.

"Ok, troops, I'm going to give you a two-hour break. There's a mess hall at Camp Viking. I have made arrangements with the Mess Sergeant to give you guys a hot meal. You guys will have to wash off as much mud as possible. The Mess Sergeant said that he wasn't going to let anyone in if they had mud all over them," he informed us.

The three of us had dropped exhausted on top of the clay bank.

"Hey, you guys, if we go back down and wash off the mud, we'll just get muddy climbing back up the bank. How about us going up and sitting on top of that bridge and drying off?" I suggested.

"Yeah, that's a good idea. We can brush each other off after we dry off," Tucker volunteered.

The three of us walked down the levee that ran alongside the canal until we reached the bridge embankment. After we had climbed up and sat on top of the bridge banister, I surveyed the area as to set my bearings. Off to the North, a short distance away from the bridge, I noticed a Vietnamese Army compound.

Just outside the encampment, two long warehouses were connected together by a lower canopy. The total structure was fabricated from corrugated tin sheets. A small lean-to with open sides supporting the same type of roof was situated between the warehouses and the river. After closer observation, I reckoned that it must serve as a kitchen since a middle-aged lady was preparing the noonday meal. A small wharf constructed from two-by-fours and warehouse pallets extended a few feet out over the river.

A young lady was sitting back on her hunches, bending over a red plastic tub. I watched as she doused the clothes a few times, then laid them out on the wooded surface of the wharf. After She had arranged the clothes to her satisfaction, she set about thrashing them with a small wooden club. After she had given them a sound thrashing she then heaped them in a pile, grabbing the plastic tub by the rim, she picked it and heaved the dirty water aside. She then refilled the tub with water, which she drew from the river in a gallon bucket. While I was standing there watching her complete the rinse cycle, I hit on a bright idea.

"Check out that girl over by the river washing clothes. Why don't we go over and ask her if we can use her washing machine?" I suggested jokingly.

"Hey! That's not a bad idea. We can dive into the water, wash ourselves off, then climb back out on top of the wharf without getting muddy again." Tucker replied joviality.

"I'm for it, and then maybe we can go to the mess hall to get some hot chow. I'm sure tired of eating C-rats; that's the only thing we've had to eat for the last two weeks," Mahoney said, agreeing with us.

The three of us set out across the thick, high grassy field that separated us from the young lady and her washing Machine. As we drew near to her, the young lady stood up and looked nervously toward the middle-aged woman in the cook shed. I walked up to her-

.trying not to stare at her breasts, which were glued to the front of a wet silk blouse. The part half-inch nipples stood out like the tops of twin mountains. God, they look good, I thought, trying to advert my gaze to her face.

"Excuse me, Miss!"I said with a big smile, trying to hide the growing bulge in front of my trousers, hoping that she wouldn't look down."Do you speak English?"

"Yes, a little bit,'" she answered, crossing her arms across her breasts, trying to hide them from view.

"My friends and I want to use this place to go into the water and wash off the mud from our uniforms. Would it be ok?"I asked.

"Yes! Yes, no sweat, please no go on wood," she said, pointing at the wharf. "American boo-cu big, wood fall in the water my papa -san be very mad with me".

"Fine, we no go wood," I replied.

"Gray, you stick around here long, and you'll be talking like she does," Tucker said with a laugh.

After a quick closer observation, I discovered that her breasts weren't the only nice things about her. The face beneath the umbrella type was strikingly beautiful. Her waist was slim enough that I could put my hands around them.

Unlike American girls, she wasn't top-heavy. Her top and bottom were of the same proportions. I glanced at Tucker and Mahoney and noticed that they were also giving her the once-over. I felt a twinge of insane jealousy, then a flood of relief, when she bent over and, picked up her washing and walked towards the warehouses.

God, I thought to myself as the three of us sat down and started pulling off our boots. I could easily fall in love with someone like her. The three of us dove into the water, uniforms and all. We even tried out the survival technique taught to us that morning, which consisted of trapping an air bubble underneath our fatigue jackets and using them for flotation devices. We swam and played around, getting most of the mud off our uniforms.

"I guess we had better get out and dry off if we are going to go and eat chow," I suggested as I pulled myself up onto the grassy riverbank. Tucker and Mahoney follow me out of the water, removing their fatigue jackets, they twist them to ring out the water.

"We had better get our asses in gear. We have only fifty minutes before we have to go back to the training course," Tucker reminded us as he spread his jacket out on the dock to dry.

The young Lady came back out; she was carrying a small plastic scrub brush in her hand.

"Give me your shirt, I show you how washee-washee," she said shyly.

I pulled off my dripping-wet fatigue jacket and handed it to her. She kneeled on wharf and bent over, dipping the jacket back in the river. She then spread the wet jacket out on the wooden boards of the dock. Picking up a bar of soap, she began to vigorously rub it on the jacket. After she had lathered the jacket throughly, she brushed it briskly with the scrub brush.

"Here, I got the idea," I said, taking the brush from her hand, with her protesting.

After I had scrubbed the jacket and rinsed it out, it had become quite clean. I then jumped back into the river to wet down my fatigue trousers, which I then washed in the same manner without removing them. I offered the washing materials to the other two guys.

"Hell! Man, I'm almost dry. I'm going to the mess hall before they stop serving Chow," said Tucker, declining the offer.

"Yeah, me too. I'm going with him. I'm starved," agreed Mahoney.

"You guys go ahead then. I'm going to wait until my clothes dry. I hate like hell to put back on a wet fatigue jacket. I'll catch up with you guys later".

"Ok, if you don't show up at the Water Survival course, we'll come back to look for you," Tucker called out as they took off back across the grassy field in the direction of the bridge.

After they had left, I sat on the bank, letting the sun slowly dry my uniform. In about ten minutes, the young lady came back out from the warehouses she was balancing two water buckets on the ends of a bamboo pole, which was slang over her right shoulder.

She walked past me and stepped up onto the dock, dropping the bucket into the river. She let it sink until only the brim and bail were showing. Like an expert fisherman, she caught the bail with the end of the pole before the bucket sank out of site. Hooking the bucket on a slot cut at the end of the pole, she pulled it from the water. After setting the bucket down on the edge of the dock she then filled the second bucket the same way.

After both buckets had been filled, she picked them up with the pole, balancing them in the same manner as before, and carried them over to a couple of fifty-five-gallon oil drums and dumped the water inside. She then came back to the river to repeat the process.

After she had refilled the buckets, I stood up.

"Here, let me give you a hand," I told her, grabbing the buckets by the bails before she could stick the pole through them.

The weight of the buckets surprised me; they were much heavier than they seemed. The young lady had lifted the weight with ease, I estimated each of the buckets weighing at least seventy-five pounds.

"Why are you filling the oil drums with water?"I inquired as I walked toward them carrying the buckets of water.

"I fill my family drink water," she replied.

"You mean your family drinks water from that river?"I said with disgust in my voice.

"Ha! Ha!" she laughed. Everyone drink water from river, even American. See that truck down by the river," she pointed towards a water purification truck that was being used to purify water for Camp Viking," It makes river water G I drank.

"I know, but it pumps water into a purification unit before we drink it," I replied.

"You see, this makes water clean so family can drink," she said, holding up a clear white-colored rock for me to inspect.

She dropped the rock into one of the oil drums that we had just filled. I looked into the other drum. The water was crystal clear, unlike the water in the first drum. She took a dipper that was hanging from the side of the drum and scooped up a dipper full of water. She drank until the dipper was half empty and slanged the remainder aside.

"Here you try; the water taste good," she refilled the dipper and handed it to me.

Not wanting to hurt her feelings, I took the dipper from her hand and took a sip. I was surprised again the water did taste much better than the water on post. I drained the dipper dry and then refilled it. As I drank another big swig, I remembered that I wasn't supposed to be drinking water from the local economy. As I took another look at the

young lady, I decided that the water must be fit to drink. She sure looked healthy enough.

"My name is Gary, What's yours?"I asked her as I handed back the dipper.

"My name Thui".

"Thui, where did you learn to speak English?"I asked.

"I finnie High School, I go work Officer Club at Dong Tam. I work for two years. GI teach me to talk Englisee.

"Are you married?"I asked.

"No! I no marry. I no have boyfriend. My father sock mal (beat) me if I go, boyfriend".

"How old are you," I asked.

"I only nineteen. I still baby-san," she replied.

"In America, almost all young girls have boyfriends, and many are married, by the time their nineteen," I told her.

Vietnam custom no same. My family pray Budda; Budda say people too young marry no lucky."

"I don't know about Buddhism, but I do agree that people who marry young don't have much luck. Too many things are against them," I replied.

"You no got wife?" she asked me.

"No, I don't have a wife or a girlfriend. I must go. It has been a pleasure talking with you, and thanks for helping me wash my uniform. I hope to meet you again sometime".

She gave me a big smile, "Yes if Budda like we meet again".

Reluctantly, I left, hoping that, indeed, I might meet the young lady again. It sure felt nice setting talking to a girl my own age. Unlike most of the guys I didn't have a girl waiting for me to come back home to. In a way, I was glad. It was enough that my mom was worrying over me, less that there be a girlfriend. I got to write to my mom the first chance I got. I thought to myself as I walked toward the front gate of Camp Viking. My musing had brought me up to the front gate. The Gate guard eyed me suspiciously as I walked through.

"Didn't you just come from those warehouses over there?" he asked me.

"Yes, I did," I answered.

"You'll get your ass in a bind. That area is off limits," he informed me.

"Whys that," I asked.

"None of us are allowed to go over to the warehouses or the ARVIN compound ever since some drunken GIs went over and tried to screw some of the ARVIN's wives. Two of them got their heads blown off. Yep, started a firefight between us and the ARVINS. Had to call some big-shot Vietnamese General out here to stop it. Ever since then, all that area has been off-limits.

"No one informed us. There's a young lady that lives in the warehouse. I sure would like to again," I replied.

"Yeah, I know. I went over there one day and tried to talk to her, but I didn't have much luck," he informed me.

I didn't bother telling him that I had carried on a long conversation with her as I left him to find the Mess Hall.

****

Chapter 3

After we had finished the jungle training courses, the three of us were assigned to "B" Company, one of the 93rd. I was assigned to the Earth Moving Platoon, which had finished their portion of the project. They were sent back to Dong Tam base camp, which gave the mechanics the opportunity to catch up on much-needed maintenance of the heavy equipment. I was assigned as a 290 operator, although I very seldom got the chance to operate one of them. They were so big and cumbersome that they weren't an effective piece of equipment to utilize in the Delta. The front blade was over ten feet wide, and they were over sixty feet long. This made it very difficult to move to job sites. Unless the company moved as a whole, they remained at Dong Tam.

Hardly two weeks had passed when we got word that the Earth Moving Platoon was to move to Camp Viking. The Reserve unit that had built the compound had been sent back to the States. I guess the compound was too nice to be turned over to the Vietnamese, so they gave it to the Engineers. The compound was much too large for our small unit. Our company of eighty enlisted men and seven officers occupied only one-quarter of the area. The CO's choice for our bivouac site was at the very center of the compound. The First Sergeant would swear that the Viet Cong were sneaking into the compound at night and sleeping in the vacant buildings. He never

Knew how close to the truth he was since a couple of NCOs had built a whorehouse in one of the empty buildings.

The compound was an ideal position to defend. A small river protected its southern border; to the north, the makeshift runway lessened the chances of sneak attacks. The most vulnerable was the stretch of high grass between the small village and the western flank. The front gate tower served as a daytime observation point and restricted access to the compound.

The bunkers were constructed on top of Air Force storage containers. Sandbagged lean-tos, constructed on top of the connexes, served as ideal observation bunker complexes. Near the center of the compound, a fifty-foot observation tower offered the advantage of a forward observation point.

I hated, like hell, as did everyone else, to pull guard in the tower. The fifty-caliber machine gun mount was the first target for Viet Cong mortar attacks. Also, the damn thing swayed every time a slight breeze stirred.

We first arrived with a skeleton crew of thirty enlisted men, seven NCOs, and two officers. All ranks of Spec. Four and below were split into two-man teams. These teams were assigned to maintain the bunkers in twelve-hour shifts. Most of us took turns pulling guard duty by ourselves during daylight hours; this would give each of us every other day off. The squad leaders were assigned to the sergeant of the guard. Their main concern was keeping us awake while on guard duty.

Sergeant Hall, our squad leader, caught us sleeping many times but, being a good sort of fellow, never reported us. If he had, our entire platoon would have been court-martialed because it was almost impossible for us to stay awake due to fatigue.

Most of the time, we manned the same bunkers. Dobly, who was my hooch mate, and I nearly always pulled guard together. We were usually assigned to the bunker in the southeast corner of the compound. This bunker overlooked the warehouses in which Thui lived. In the afternoons, I would watch her come to the river to do her domestic chores. As the sun began to set, she would move into the kitchen area to help her mother prepare the evening meal. I noticed that she had a lot of brothers and sisters; this being the case, she was continuously washing clothes. As I watched her through my binoculars, I began to fall in love with her from afar. After the day that I had gone over to wash off the mud from my uniform, I had never gathered the courage to return. One reason was that the area was off-limits, and the other was that I was a little shy. One evening, while I was watching her go about her evening chores, Dobly became interested in her.

"Hey Gary, give me those binoculars for a minute. I want to see what's so interesting over there that you're all the time watching," he said.

"Here, take a look at that girl over by the river," I said as I handed him the binoculars.

He took them from me and focused them on Thui, who was squatting over another tub of clothes.

"Hey! She's a looker. I'm going over tomorrow to see her," he said.

I grabbed the binoculars out of his hands. "You duck head, I saw her first; she's mine!"I told him with a twinge of jealousy in my voice.

"She's just another gook. You're not going to marry her," he retorted.

"No one knows what the future holds. You just can't ever tell. I think she's the most beautiful girl I have ever seen. Yeah! I would marry her," I replied.

"What! Man, are you crazy? When was the last time you had a piece of ass? What would your mother say if you brought a gook home," he said to me as if disgusted at the thought.

That ended the conversation. He had asked me a few questions that I had no answer for, and I wasn't about to tell him that I had never made love before. That was just one thing you didn't admit to another soldier. I had gotten away with claiming that I didn't have any protection the last time we all had stopped at the local whorehouse.

"Gary, you don't have a girlfriend back home?"Dobly asked me as he climbed on top of the row of sandbags and leaned back against the corner post.

"Not really. I know a few that said they would write me when I went off to basic training, but I never did hear from any of them," I replied.

"Here's my girl." she pulled his wallet out of his pocket and unwrapped it from a waterproof pouch.

"We're going to get married as soon as I get back home," he said, showing me a picture of a pretty, typical blonde, blue-eyed Midwest beauty.

"What kind of car do you have?" I asked, trying to change the subject.

"I haven't bought one yet. I'm going to buy one as soon as I get back to the world. Yep, I'm going right down and buying me a new vet. How about you?"

"I've got a '67 GTO. I'm letting my younger brother drive it until I get back home."I replied.

We sat and talked about girls, cars, football, and high school until it was nearly midnight. Dobly pulled out a joint and lit it up.

"You want a drag?" he asked, passing the joint over to me.

"Nah, it doesn't do anything for me when I smoke them," which was another excuse I had thought up to keep guys from coaxing me into smoking marijuana.

"You'd better take a hit; it'll help you relax. Anyway, it's your turn to get some shut-eye."

"No thanks, I'm going to get some sleep. Wake me up if you get sleepy," I said, again declining his offer.

An uneasy feeling aroused me from an uncomfortable sleep. I sat up instinctively, reaching for my M-16, but it wasn't in the usual place I kept it. I groped around the dark confines of the bunker; still, I couldn't locate my weapon. The hair on the back of my neck was standing up, and goosebumps were running up and down my arms. A cold sweat broke out as I frantically went over and tried to shake Dobly from a sound sleep.

"Hey, Dobly! Wake up! Wake up, you hear?"I said in a low whisper, shaking him hard enough to rattle his teeth.

"What's wrong?" he asked, sitting up and groggily wiping the sleep from his eyes.

"Where's your weapon," I asked him.

"Here it is," he answered while groping around in the dark for it.

"Hey man, it's not here! What did you do with it?" he asked me.

"Mine's missing too. Someone came up and relieved us of them," I said with anxiety.

"It was a VC sniper. He's probably waiting for us to stand up so he can blow our heads off with them," he explained to me excitedly.

Hurriedly, he rolled off the top of the sandbags and hunched down behind them. Slowly, he raised up, trying to peer over the top of the sandbags.

"Do you see anything," he asked.

"You're looking in the wrong direction. If it had been the VC, they would have cut our throats," I informed him.

"Maybe they didn't have knives, and our weapons were the only things they were after," he replied.

The reasoning was a probability but highly unlikely.

"What do you think happened to them," he asked me worriedly.

"I have no idea, but we had better radio Sergeant Hall and tell him," I suggested.

"God, I hate to do that. He has already caught me sleeping two times; he's gonna be mad as hell," he replied.

"I know, but it's the only thing we can do," I suggested.

About thirty minutes after I had called Sergeant Hall, I saw the blackout lights of a Jeep coming down the lane in our direction. The Jeep pulled to a stop in front of the bunker. Sergeant Hall got out of the Jeep carrying two M-16s. He made his way up the wooden ladder and came inside the bunker.

"Here are you guys, some more weapons. You'll have to report the other two missing to the Platoon Sergeant first thing in the morning. He'll have to make out a report. You guys will be lucky if you don't get Article 15," he said as he handed the weapons to us.

"Shit," I said.

I didn't mind getting Article 15 as much as I did having to face Sergeant Winfield, our platoon sergeant.

"Anyway, how did you guys manage to let your weapons get stolen?"

"I don't know, Sarge we must have dozed off. Then someone climbed up and took them," Dobly answered.

"Having you two guys on guard will sure make me sleep soundly," he said sarcastically.

"See if you guys can stay awake for the rest of the night," he told us as he climbed back down the ladder and got back in his Jeep.

I was still sweating, even though the night air was chilling. We sat saying nothing as we watched the Jeep's rear blackout markers disappear back down the lane. Now, we were in one hell of a predicament. One of us would have to go down and see if our Claymores had been turned around on us. That would be the first thing a sapper would do. I wasn't too worried about satchel charges; they usually had timing devices that caused them to detonate seconds after they were thrown.

"I'll go down and check the Claymores," I volunteered as I picked up one of the M-16s. It felt somewhat familiar to my touch. After six months of sleeping and eating with the damn thing, I knew every little nick and cut on the stock and handguard.

"Dobly, let me see your cigarette lighter," I requested.

He fished it out of his trouser pocket as I pulled out my wallet and unwrapped it from its waterproof bag.

"Here you go," he said, handing me the lighter as I slipped my info card out of my wallet.

I struck the lighter and held it up close to the serial number stamped on the side of the weapon and then checked it against the number on the info card, the numbers matched.

"Damn! Just as I thought," I said

"Why? What's wrong," Dobly asked.

"Check the serial number on that other weapon, and you'll see."

"It wouldn't do any good. I don't know what my serial number is. I'm not really sure that the weapon I had was even mine. We get them mixed up when we go out on the job sites. We pile them all together in a pile. When we finish working, we just grab the first weapon we come to," he explained.

"Well! One thing's for sure: this is the weapon that I was issued. Sergeant Hall must have climbed up here and caught us both asleep and took our weapons to teach us a lesson. Hell! He was going to let us turn ourselves into the platoon sergeant by letting us report them missing."

"What the hell are we going to do now? Do you think he will turn us into Sergeant Winfield?" he asked worriedly.

"I don't know, but one thing's for sure. I learned a hell of a lesson. Lucky thing for us, it wasn't the Viet Cong. If it had been, we'd be lying here breathing through our throats. That will be the last time anyone ever catches me asleep while on guard duty."

"I'll agree with you. Sergeant Hall told me that both of us were in for promotion to Spec Four. If he turns us in, the LT will tear up our orders. I was going to save the extra money to buy me that new Vette," he said, shaking his head worriedly.

"It would have been nice getting the extra money. It's one hundred and thirty more a month. I don't think Sergeant Hall will

report us as long as he doesn't catch us sleeping again," I told him, trying to reassure him.

The seriousness of our incompetence was well embedded in both our minds. It was the first and last time that I ever disregarded duties of any type.

Days and nights began to rush by. As other platoons finished their portions of the bridge-building project, more men were assigned to guard duties. Soon, we had enough men that we only had to pull guard every three days. This made it a lot easier for everyone concerned. I was lying asleep when one afternoon, Dobly came in and woke me.

"Gary, wake your ass up. You've got to chip in ten dollars to hire a housemaid," he said as he shook us awake.

That sounded good to me. All this time, I had been shining my own boots and making my own bed. I had to get one of the other hooch's housemaids to do my laundry.

"When is she going to start?"I asked.

"She'll be starting tomorrow morning. The operations sergeant hired her," he informed me.

I got up and gave him the ten dollars. It was time for me to prepare to go on guard duty. It would be nice to have our own hooch maid. I thought as I sat down to brush a shine on my boots, how I hated shining the damn things. Usually, I paid the other hooch's housemaid to shine them for me. A lot of times, she was too busy and couldn't get around to doing it. There were six of us living in the hooch: PFC Dobly, Spec Four King, PFC Kraber, Spec Four Willift, myself, and our hooch commander, Sergeant Hall. All of us got along very well, although it did get perplexing at times, especially when record players were playing three kinds of music at the same time. It was very seldom that all of us were in the hooch at the same time. The

platoon sergeant tried to arrange our duties so that one of us was left to guard the hooch.

The most annoying thing about pulling guard duty was trying to sleep the next day. Our hooch was the hottest of them all. The canvas top trapped the heat, turning it into a sauna. It was utterly impossible to sleep without a fan. I had finished another night of guard duty and was lying on top of my bunk with the fan blowing over a chunk of ice I had stolen from the mess hall. I had drifted off to sleep when a gentle shake and a soft voice awakened me.

"Excuse me, excuse me, wake up please," the voice was telling me.

I opened my eyes, blinked, then closed them again. I must be having a dream, I thought to myself. I slowly opened my eyes again.

There, looking down at me, was that beautiful face that I had been observing through my binoculars for the past three months.

"I new hooch maid," the soft voice said. Sergeant Hall say me wake you up. He says you show me all man's clothes. I go washee-washee them," she informed me.

My heart started racing wildly, and a lump came in my throat, making it difficult for me to talk.

"Thui! You are Thui, aren't you?"I managed to ask, still disbelieving.

She gasped and covered her mouth in astonishment. "You know my name. How you know my name? I never see you before," her astonishment turned to nervous caution.

"You may not remember me, but I remember you well."

. "I go wash clothes; you show me clothes," She gave me a puzzled look.

"You are supposed to clean the hooch and makeup beds first. When you're done, you can shine your boots and wash clothes," I instructed her.

"Ok, I take boots over here, make shine," she pointed to a vacant corner of the hooch.

"I'll be right back; I'm going to go take a shower."I grabbed a towel and my shaving kit and headed out the door in the direction of the showers. I hurried through my morning bathing, anticipating returning back and becoming better acquainted with Thui. For the first time since I had arrived in Vietnam, I was in high spirits. I even started whistling a tune as I lathered myself down. I just couldn't believe my good fortune. Fate had finally come my way. When I returned to the hooch, she had nearly finished shining my boots. I walked back and picked up the one she had already finished.

"Before, I think the American army had lots of money. Now I see you just same-same Vietnam army," she said as she handed me the other boot.

"What do you mean by saying that," I asked.

"You boot too big for you feet, Vietnam army same-same," she explained.

"No, you're wrong. That is the right size boot. I just have big feet," I informed her.

She walked over and picked up one of the other boots that she was going to start to polish and set it down beside my footed boot.

"See, you boot two boot, I polish one, you boot, you pay for two boot," she complained.

"What? A bald-headed man doesn't get a discount when he gets a haircut," I said jokingly.

"That's different. I use too much polish; I make shine, you boot," she complained.

"Ok, I'll tell you what I'll do, you shine my boots, and I'll buy the polish. Is that a deal?"

She looked at my size fourteens and shook her head, "Ok, but my arm get tired two time more," she said, quite pleased with her negotiations.

As she sat back on her hunches, spreading boot black on the rest of the boots, she kept giving me shy little glances.

"How you know my name," she asked shyly.

"Do you remember, about four months ago, three GIs came to your dock and washed the mud from their uniforms," I asked her.

A flicker of recollection crossed her face, which broke into a delightful smile.

"Ok! I know you. You help me carry water. You tell me you live at Dong Tam."

"I did, at that time. Our company moved here, a short time after that," I explained.

"Why you not come see my house?" she asked me with a shy, hurt voice.

"I was afraid of your father before you told me he'd get mad if anyone came calling on you."

"You no afraid of my father, you be nice man, he likes you."

"Thui, I'm going to the Mess Hall. I'll be right back. Did you bring anything to eat?"

"No, I work finish, I go home, I eat," she said, refusing the food.

"I'll see if I can scrape up something and bring it back to you," I told her.

She turned up her aristocratic nose in detest, "Thank you, no, I go home, I eat," she insisted.

"Why don't you like American food," I asked.

"Yes, but I no eat garbage can food; it make me sick," she replied.

"What are you talking about? I'm not going to bring you food from the garbage."I assured her.

"You say you going to scrape up food and bring for me to eat," she insisted.

"Ha-ha! That was just American slang. What I really mean, is that I was going to try to bring you back a tray of food," I explained.

"Oh! Thank you! I'm sorry, I now understand," she apologized with an embarrassed giggle.

"I'll be right back," I said as I bent over and scooped my boonie hat from the top of my bunk and slapped it on top of my head.

I opened the screen door with an intube tension strip to keep it closed as I stepped out onto the wooden catwalk. I noticed Dobly coming out from the Camp Cub, a few hooches down.

"Gary! Hey Gary! Look what I got," he called out, gleefully waving a paper.

"I got my traveling orders; also, our spec four orders came in. Serge says for you to stop by his hooch and pick up your stripes, he informed me.

"Did you meet our new hooch maid," I inquired after he stopped talking.

"No, not yet; Sergeant Hall said she was a looker; I'm on my way to talk her out of a piece of pussy. Take your time about getting back," he said with a stupid grin.

"Ok, you ass hole! You had better keep your cotton-picking hands off her. She's Thui, the girl that lives in those warehouses across from the front gate," I warned him.

"Hey! She's fair game as long as she is working for us Americans," he retorted as he walked in the direction of our hooch.

"Fuck head! You had better pay attention to what I'm telling you, or I'll kick your ass when I get back from chow," I called out angrily after him.

I walked onto the chow hall, worried and angry. What if Dobly messed with her and scared her into going home, I mused. Damn, asshole! I sure would hate it if she left even before I had the chance to know her better.

Angrily, I kicked the sandbags at the corner of the mess hall. I opened the door and entered; the chow line had thinned down to only a couple of troops. I grabbed a couple of trays and slid them down the rail that ran in front of the serving line. The grubby, overweight mess sergeant, who was standing just behind the cooks serving line, eyed me suspiciously.

"Hey, troop, where are you headed with two trays?" he asked.

"I have to take a tray down to the bunker beside the front gate. The CO added a new position to the daytime guard roster," I lied.

"Damn! You mean I have to send another tray out to those bunkers? Between the NCOs stealing the coffee cups and the troops carrying the trays off to their hooches, we don't have any damn dishes as it is," he grumbled.

"Don't worry, Sarge. I'll be personally responsible to see that the tray gets back," I assured him.

"I'll believe it when I see it," he replied.

I was quite pleased with myself as I carried the trays back to the hooch. I should be able to chalk up some points now, I thought as I pushed the screen door open by backing through it. The hooch was empty except for Dobly, who was stretched out on top of his bunk, boots propped up on the rail, and fingers laced behind his head.

"Hey, good, you brought me a tray," he said, sitting up on the edge of the bunk.

"It's not for you; it's for Thui. She didn't bring any lunch to work with her," informed him.

"Ah, give it here; she won't be needing it. She didn't want to fuck, so I told her to get her ass out of here and go home," he answered back.

A red film of anger slowly clouded my senses. I was angrier than I had ever been in my entire life. I threw the trays aside and hurled myself across the distance between us, grabbing him by his throat. I lifted him up off the bunk. I was determined to keep him from drawing any air; my hands began to slowly squeeze the life from him. His face had turned purple, his tongue was protruding, and he had stopped kicking me when I finally came back to my senses.

"You fucking bastard!"I shouted, tossing him back down on the bunk and banging his head against the railing.

"You're just like all the rest of the GIs over here. You don't give a damn bit of respect for anyone. You had better hope that I can go and talk her into coming back. If she doesn't, I just might come back and finish the job," I warned him.

By now, a little color had returned to his face, and he stopped coughing. He sat back up, rubbing the deep red finger marks that I had left on his throat.

"Damn! Gary, I thought you was kidding about being in love with that girl. Shit! Man, you almost killed me," he said hoarsely.

"Listen, you little fuck, it doesn't matter what I feel about her. You just can't go around mistreating women just because they wouldn't screw you," I replied, still mad as hell.

"Hey man, I'm sorry. If you can get her to come back, I'll apologize to her and promise not to fuck with her anymore."

I left the hooch still mad as hell but glad that I hadn't choked him to death. As I walked down the dusty lane that led to the front gate, I began to cool off somewhat. As I neared the front gate, a sickening feeling crept to the top of my stomach. What if she doesn't want to come back? I really couldn't blame her. The more I thought about it, the more ashamed I became. Now, I was starting to regret having attacked Dobly. Deep down inside, I knew that my intentions weren't any more honorable than his. The only difference was that I was willing to work a little slower and be more subtle.

I spoke to the gate guard as I walked through the front gate.

"Hey man, I'll be right back, I got to go over to those warehouses and speak to our hooch maid," I assured him.

He looked up from the makeshift desk at which he was sitting and gave a nod. I ducked under the guard rail and made my way across the gravel road that lay between the gate and the warehouses. I didn't know where to enter, but on numerous occasions, I had observed people entering through a side entrance. I decided to give the entrance a try. Nervously, I walked through the veranda and entered the warehouse, which gave me the impression of being the family living area. Ten-foot poles supported the raised hinged sides, letting the cool afternoon breeze blow through. Two knee-high, six-by-eight-foot tables lined each side of the warehouse. Later I was to learn that these were the bedrooms. I glanced around but didn't see anyone stirring about. Not wishing to venture further into the warehouse, I stopped at the end of the tables.

"Thui! Thui!"I called out, my nervous voice quivering from the lump stuck in my throat.

I heard a flood of Vietnamese behind me. I turned around in time to ward off a blow from a short-handled rice straw broom, which was coming at the side of my head. Before I had time to recover, the broom swung down and caught me above the rib cage. Realizing that I would not be able to ward off the blows that were coming at me as fast as machine-gun bullets, I became determined to try throwing my arms around the five feet of mad, raging fury and try to hold down the arms before they could do any more damage. In the process, I received a couple more stinging blows to the side of my head before I had the screaming Vietnamese subdued.

About this time, Thui appeared through the open doorway that led to the other side of the warehouse. She said something to the Vietnamese lady, who stopped struggling in my arms.

"Is it okay for me to let go of her?"I asked apprehensively. Thui began laughing and trying to apologize at the same time.

"My mother think you bad GI, who try to slickie make love to me," she explained.

"It's a good thing that you were here to stop her before she beat me to death with that broom. Tell her that in America, we have a saying, 'The first impression is a lasting impression," I told her.

"What does that mean? I don't understand all English words," she asked.

"It means is that what a person does or says the first time you meet them is the way you'll always remember them. The way I will remember your mother is never to make her mad at me," I explained to her.

She relayed what I had told her mother. The woman said something to Thui again in Vietnamese.

"My mother says she very sorry, she much ashamed, she happy to meet you," Thui interrupted for her mother.

"Tell her don't worry about it, that I was very angry at the GI that bothered you also. That's what I came to talk to you about. I found out from Dobly, the GI that bothered you, what had happened. He said that he wouldn't bother you again if you would reconsider coming back to work."

"I don't think my mother will let me. She very nervous GI. She worry GI slickie make love to me; I no can marry," she explained.

"Please talk to her again and tell her that I will watch you and not let anyone bother you anymore," I promised.

"Ok, I ask her, but I no think she let me go back to GI compound."

They talked it over for a while; it seemed as though they were arguing. As I listened, my need to learn Vietnamese became more manifest. How I wished I had the ability to reassure Thui's mom and let her know that I wouldn't let anything happen to Thui. After about ten minutes of serious argument, Thui's mother finally gave in.

"My mother no like I go work for American. I talk her my family need money; I tell her I big girl I can take care myself. Before I work Dong Tam, no, thing happen to me. She say if you promise your word you no let GI slickie make love me, she give me go back work."

I didn't know exactly how to reassure Thui's mother, so I did what I had seen a Vietnamese soldier do when confronted by one of his superiors. I clasped my fists in my open palm, held them out in front of me, and bowed awkwardly at the waist. This must have been the right move, for she broke into a big grin, grabbed my hand, and led me over to one of the four tables that had been set up just beyond the benches. Thui followed us over and sat down across from me. Her mom went behind a counter and brought me out a bottle of coke and set it down in front of me, making motions for me to drink.

"I think my mother like you. She tell me that you have a kind face and clear eyes that don't lie. She say you stay she fix you food, you eat," she relayed to me.

As her mother scurried about behind the counter, busy preparing food, Thui and I sat and chatted. I tried hard to think up some way that I could ask her out on a date. The only thing that I could think of was taking her on base to see a movie. I would have to get permission from the First Sergeant to accomplish this. To hell with that idea; I knew that the First Sergeant wouldn't go for a PFC bringing his hooch maid back on base after hours. I knew that if I tried, it would be inviting trouble for Thui and me. I'll leave it up to Thui and see what kind of idea she can come up with, I thought to myself. Wait a minute, Gray, you're getting way ahead of yourself; she might not even want to go on a date with you, I told myself.

"Thui, what do young Vietnamese do when they go out on a date," I asked.

She laughed nervously, "Why are you asking me out on a date," she inquired.

"I think it would be pleasant for the two of us to go to a Vietnamese restaurant, eat dinner, then go catch a movie," I answered.

"Yes, I would like that very much, but first, you will have to meet my father. We go to a restaurant to eat, you ask my mother and father to go to, ok?"

"That would be just fine with me. How many brothers and sisters do you have," I asked.

"I have three brothers and four sisters. The two young ones stay home; all others go to school. They come home at five o'clock this afternoon. I call my brother and sister, come here, you meet them, OK?" She asked of me.

She got up and, went back to the warehouse, and disappeared behind the partition that separated the warehouse. All hell broke as soon she reappeared dragging two screaming, kicking kids by their arms. Reacting as I would if they were American children, I stood up and reached for the one closest to me. This was a mistake; they each reached a higher note of screaming, twisting away from Thui, making a beeline straight back to the open door of the warehouse.

"They very much afraid of Americans," Thui explained. "They say you try to steal them. I say no, you nice American. They ask if you nice American, why Mother hit you with broom?."

"Ha! Ha!"I laughed.

"I hope that their impression of me doesn't last too long. The next time I go to the PX, I will buy some candy and bring it back to them. Most kids are easily bribed," I assured her.

By this time, Thui's mother had finished preparing the food. She brought over two steaming bowls of noodle soup, which gave off an appetizing odor, making me realize I had missed breakfast and lunch.

"That was really good, I told Thui after finishing off the bowl of noodle soup. Tell your mother I said thank you," I requested.

"I teach you to say thank you in Vietnamese. You tell her, she be very happy. Say to her, "Cam Un Kneul Lam, My Oie," she taught me.

After practicing the line a few times, I finally got the hang of it. After Thui's mother had finally got the two screaming kids quiet, she came back from the other room. I told her what Thui had taught me to say. For some reason, it really did make her happy.

"What did I say to her?" I asked Thui.

"You said, 'Thank you, mother.' See, I tell you say, she be more happy," she told me gleefully.

"That's great! I have made lots of points with her. I hope I can make some with father when I meet him."

"Thui, I have to go back to the compound. I'll come to the front gate to pick you up bright and early tomorrow morning," I informed her.

"Chau Ba," I said to her mother, the only words I knew in Vietnamese.

"Thank you for coming and talking to my mother. I think she feels much better now."

****

Chapter 4

In the days that followed, Thui and I began the slow process of falling deeply in love. I would meet her at the front gate and walk with her to our hooch. It soon became known to everyone that we were lovers. I knew that my friends didn't approve; they would stop in the middle of conversations as soon as I walked up to them. Once, I overheard a conversation between two of my hooch mates. I had just returned from chow and was about to push the screen door up to enter the hooch. I stopped short when I heard my and Thui's names mentioned.

"Hey, the crazy bastard's in love with her. Dobly told me, the night before he went back to the States, that he tried to kill him with his bare hands after he caught him trying to screw her."

"Yeah, I know," the other person replied. "Dobly also informed me... Hell, I'm scared to say anything to her. If she weren't doing such a good job of cleaning and washing my clothes, I'd tell Sergeant Hall to get rid of her. I'd hate like hell to have that big son of a bitch mad at me. Hell, I've seen him lift up five-ton dump tires over his head and toss them up onto the back of a dump truck."

"Yeah, I'd sure hate like hell to make that big son of a bitch mad at me."

Quietly, I backtracked down the boarded sidewalk until I was a short distance outside the hooch. I walked up to the hooch, scuffing my boots loudly on the walkway. They ended their conversation abruptly as I entered the hooch.

"Are you going to visit Thui tonight," Sessions asked me as he flipped up a card from the deck he was holding and tossed it on top of the army blanket that was spread over the top of a footlocker.

"No, I have only been to her house one time. Her father is not too hip to Americans, so I'm a little leery about going over."

"Good, then pull up a chair and play a game of seven-card draw with us."

"Okay, but not too long. I'm not too good at the game; most of the time, I only contribute."

"Ah, come on. We'll take it easy on you," begged Mercer, taking a look at his hand and disgustedly tossing them onto the middle of the blanket. "Maybe you'll change my luck," he said doubtfully.

"Okay, deal me in the next hand. How much are you guys playing for anyway," I asked.

"Ah, this is just a small game—nickel, a dime, quarter limit," Mercer answered in reply.

I pulled up a chair and played a few hands with them, losing all of them.

"Gary, if I ask you something, you promise not to get pissed off and whip my ass," Sessions asked as he dealt us another round of cards?

"That all depends," I answered, picking up my hand and glancing at the cards I had been dealt. "I don't think anything could piss me off more than this hand does."

"How do you feel about GIs marrying gooks and taking them back to the world," he asked?

"No more than I feel about GIs marrying Specs, Dagos, Chinks, or Japs that are already there. If they love each other, it's none of anyone else's business. Furthermore, as for anyone moving to

America because of its great opportunities, it seems to me that none of us would be here if our forefathers hadn't made that decision," I answered.

"What would your mother and father say if you brought a gook home," he inquired?

"I don't have to worry about what my mother and father would say. What I have to worry about is what assholes like you will say," I replied, angrily tossing the cards back down on the locker and springing to my feet. The chair that I was sitting in went flying backward as I reached over and grabbed a handful of T-shirts, ripping it down the front as it tore loose from his body. He crawled backward over his bunk, trying to put it in between us.

"Hey, remember you said that you wouldn't get pissed if I asked you," he begged as he crouched behind his bunk.

The anger left as suddenly as it came. "I said that it all depends on the question. We have to make some rules around here. I can't go beating up everyone that pisses me off. First of all, if you guys are really and truly my friends, then you have to respect the fact that I don't look at everyone the way you guys do. I don't like to hear ethnic groups referred to as Specs, Dagos, Chinks, or gooks, especially someone that I care deeply for. So, I would appreciate it if you didn't call them those names when you're around me," I informed them.

"Okay, then what do we call niggers?" Sessions asked, knowing that I was from Arkansas and that was the derogatory name we referred to the Black race.

"You can add them to the list too. I never did like that name, either. If you can't ask a person their name, then why bother with or about them," I replied.

I felt the need for some fresh air and stepped outside into the night air. I wandered around the boardwalks until I found myself next to the commo bunker. The commo specialist was standing in the doorway smoking a cigarette, which he hurriedly put out when he heard my approach. I walked up to him and asked him how everything was.

"It was just fine until you sneaked up on me and caused me to put out my joint," he replied, bending down and searching the area around his feet for what was left of the joint.

"What brings you out this way," he asked as he lit his lighter to try to relight his marijuana cigarette.

"Here, you want a hit," he held out the joint to me.

"No thanks, you go ahead. Don't let me bother you; I'm just walking around trying to clear my head."

"Why, what's wrong," he asked.

He drew a deep breath of smoke into his lungs and held it for a few seconds. He exploded into a coughing frenzy that sounded like he was trying to cough up his lungs.

"YOU wouldn't understand," I told him.

"Try me. This dope brings out the philosopher in me," he sucked in another long breath of smoke, getting the same reaction as he had from the first one.

"Damn, man, do you have to do that to get high off that stuff?"I asked him.

"Hey man, are you telling me that you've never tried this stuff," he replied, holding out the remainder of the joint to me.

"I said I didn't want anything to do with that stuff," I replied angrily, turning to walk away.

"Hey man, come back and talk. I'll put this out," he called out after me. Maybe the guy's not as bad as he seems, I thought. I need to talk to someone. If he's messed up from smoking dope, maybe he'll not remember what we talked about, I thought as I turned around and walked back up to him.

"It's not much. I think I'm in love," I replied.

"Can't eat, can't sleep, feels like a large knot growing in the bottom of your stomach?"

"Yeah, you're right. How do you know?"

"I was the same way a few months back. It went away after I asked her to marry me, and she agreed."

"Asked who to marry you?"

"My girlfriend. She lives down in the village. I'm doing the paperwork to take her back to the States with me."

"How do you start?"

"First, you have to get the CO's permission to marry her, which is the hardest. She has to have a background investigation. I've been working on the paperwork for eighteen months. I don't know if I will get it finished in time. We had a Buddhist wedding already, but the government doesn't recognize it. We still have to get the CO's permission and be married by a chaplain before I can get permission to take her back to the States."

"I haven't asked her to marry me as of yet," I replied. "Have you slept with her yet?"

"No, not yet," I replied.

"I didn't think so. Any Vietnamese girl with any class won't let you screw her until they have a marriage certificate in their hands. If she does, she's no different from any of the whores that you can pick up in the back alleys of My Tho. When are you going to ask her to marry you?"

"Right now. You talked me into it. I'm going to sneak out the front gate and go ask her."

"Where does she live," he asked.

"In those warehouses just outside the front gate."

"You mean Thui? She's my wife's best friend, so you're the guy she's always talking about. She told my wife that she really likes you a lot. If you expect to get into her pants before you get married, forget it. She's a cherry girl. Also, you'll have to get on her father's good side, and going there to see her after dark sure isn't the way to do it. You will have to get Thui to tell him that she wants to invite you to dinner. One other thing—don't ever let him see you hold or kiss her. It would be a good idea to take him a bottle of Hennessy cognac when you visit. It'll impress him a lot."

"I'm sure glad I stopped by to talk to you. I feel much better already."

"Yeah, me too. It's good to know that someone else has been bitten by the bug, too. One more thing: keep everything to yourself. If the platoon sergeant or the CO gets wind of you trying to marry a Vietnamese, he'll send you up north to one of the engineer units building QL One."

"How the hell am I going to get permission to marry if I don't ask him?"

"If Thui agrees to marry you, I'll give you the address of a Vietnamese lawyer in My Tho who'll do the paperwork. Even then, it'll take you eight to ten months to get a Vietnamese marriage license. If you get a Vietnamese marriage license first, then the Army will have to let you do the paperwork to get married legally.

"It sounds pretty hard to me."

"It is; you have to be very determined. I've put up with all kinds of hell ever since I started the paperwork. I should be a Staff Sergeant already, but the CO makes up things that get me busted. If you expect to marry a Vietnamese, you can kiss any kind of an Army career goodbye. My wife's going to have a baby within the next couple of

months. I just hope that I can get all the paperwork done before I DEROS back to the States," he informed me.

"I wish you luck. If there's anything I can do, let me know. When Thui comes into work tomorrow morning, I'm going to ask her to marry me."I answered.

"Stop by and keep me informed," he said

I walked back to my hooch. It was as if a great burden had been lifted. I sure was glad that I had talked to Specialist List; at least now I knew what Thui's feelings were about me. The hooch was empty when I returned, so I figured everyone must be down at the camp club. At least I wouldn't have to talk to any of them. I have got to be a little more careful and not get into a fight with some stupid jackass, and I thought to myself as I turned back my bedroll and climbed into bed. At least I had tomorrow off, and I would get the chance to talk to Thui, I thought as I drifted off into the first peaceful sleep since I had joined the Army.

I was awakened by something tickling my nose. Half-asleep, I tried to brush it away. It was then I heard a girlish giggle. I opened my eyes in time to catch Thui slipping a piece of broom straw back under my nose. I reached out fast and grabbed her, drawing her to me. She tried halfheartedly to get away from my embrace but stopped squirming as I sought her lips and planted a long kiss on them. She surprised me by parting her lips and seeking my tongue with hers. She drew away from me suddenly, embarrassed by her brashness.

"What a wonderful way to be awakened," I told her as I swung my feet around to the plywood floor.

She had picked up a load of clothes and started out the rear door of the hooch. I hurried, put my trousers on, and called out to her through the screen door.

"Thui! Wait a minute; I want to talk to you before you get too busy."I requested.

She set the load of clothes down on the ground and re-entered the hooch.

"Come sit by me for a minute; I want to talk to you," I said, patting the bunk.

Shyly, she came over and sat down beside me.

"What would your family think if you were to marry an American," I asked.

"My mother no care, but I think my father get very angry," she replied.

"Good, at least I will have one person on my side. The reason I asked is that I have fallen in love with you and want to ask you to marry me."

She covered her hand with her mouth in shocked dismay and jumped up from the bunk.

"I sorry, I like you very much and think you very nice man, but I no sleep with you. If you need woman, I tell my father take you go see Cong De Nhieu girl."

"No! You're wrong. That's not what I want. I respect you very much. I don't want to sleep with you until we are married and have the papers to take you back to America," I replied.

She rushed me and threw her arms around me, nearly bowling me off the bunk with the force.

"I so happy; I, too, feel love with you for a long time. I like to marry you, go to America, but first, we have to have my father say OK. Maybe take a long time. How long you go back to America?"

"I have four more months left, but don't worry about that. I am going to put in for a six-month extension today. If that doesn't give us enough time, I can re-enlist for Vietnam."

"For sure, you love me enough to do that for me," she asked studying my face to see if she could tell if I was lying to her or not.

"If I love you, what else can I do,"?

"We have to be very careful until I get the extension approved. We only act like good friends. If the First Sergeant or CO finds out about us, he won't approve the paperwork."I suggested.

"Yes, I know. I go now, washee washee uniforms. Later I come back, we talk some more about marry, OK," she said as she went outside.

I slipped my boots and fatigue jacket on and walked up to the orderly room. As I walked along the familiar boardwalk, I mused deeply in my thoughts. The "what ifs" were racing across my mind. I had witnessed the disgust and contempt that most Americans had for the Vietnamese. I knew the road ahead of me would be rough and rocky, but I had no idea of the difficulties the next few months would bring. I opened the door to the orderly room and stepped inside. The First Sergeant was sitting at his desk, smoking one of those damn cigars that had become synonymous with him. Choking for breath, I walked up to his desk.

"What the hell can I do for you, Gray?" he asked, blowing smoke across his desk toward my face.

"If you came looking for your DEROS orders, you're too early. You still have sixty days before they'll be cut," he informed me.

"No, First Sergeant, that's not the reason I'm here. I want to fill out the paperwork for a six-month extension."

"What? Man, have you been drinking? Everyone I know is trying to get the hell out of this place. You'd better have a good reason for wanting to extend, and it had better not be to start paperwork to marry a Vietnamese. Like the reason I got last month. I saved that guy's life by notifying the battalion commander and getting him sent home the next week. I'm sure he's thanking me just about now while he's sitting in the NCO club sipping on a cold beer."

"No, that's not my reason. I will have only nine months left when I return to the States. I would like to stay in Nam, hoping that I will make E-5 before I go back." Appealing to his softer qualities, I added, "Just in case I decide to reenlist."

"Well, that sounds like a good enough reason to me," he said. "I'll get the company clerk to type up the necessary papers. You can come back later and sign them."

I was feeling light-hearted and uplifted as I made my way back down the boardwalk to my hooch. As soon as my request for an extension was approved, I planned to start the paperwork to get permission to marry. I just couldn't wait to get back and tell Thui the good news! We had to start making plans. It shouldn't take over thirty to forty-five days, I was thinking. In the meantime, I had to win Thui's father over so that we could get his permission. I could start by getting one of the NCOs that I didn't drink with to go to the exchange and buy a bottle of whiskey for me.

One has to be an NCO and twenty-one years old to purchase hard liquor at the exchange. Maybe I could get SSgt Skeet to buy one for me. I thought to myself as I opened the screen door to my hooch and stepped inside. Staff Sergeant was our assistant platoon sergeant and poker game partner. I made a mental note to speak to him about it later that afternoon.

During the first few weeks of our whirlwind romance, I took much time to reconsider my passion for Thui. Did I love her because of my situation, or was my love the real genuine thing? This was a hard question for a nineteen-year-old kid; it is also a hard question for me to answer today. The only thing that I knew was that I had never felt so strongly for anyone in my entire life, which gave me the determination to be with Thui for the rest of my life. Although lots of anxieties did arise: How would my parents react to my marrying Thui? Would she be able to adjust to being away from her family? As I brought these questions up to her, she kept telling me the same thing. She would follow me anywhere that I went.

"I no like to go America; I may not see my family ever again, but you be my husband, and no like to stay Vietnam. I go America too," she said to me one afternoon while we were sitting on a bench beside the front gate.

"Thui, when are we going to tell your parents that we are getting married? I got Sergeant Skeet to buy a bottle of Hennessy cognac, which I am going to give him as a peace offering. Maybe we can all meet somewhere, like a restaurant, and then I'll ask him for his permission to marry you."

"That good idea. If he no like, he no yell at me till I go home," she replied.

"Tomorrow is Saturday, and we don't have to work in the afternoon. How about we plan for tomorrow afternoon?"

"Okay, I tell my parents that you would like to go eat Vietnamese food. You come to my house at four o'clock; we all go to the restaurant together. I hire a taxi to come take us."

"Sounds good to me. You go on home; I am going to catch a ride to Dong Tam. I need to buy some things from the PX. I will come to your house at three forty-five tomorrow."

****

Chapter 5

When she awakened the next morning, her father had already taken the family bicycle and gone to report to the province chief. This was his regular routine every Saturday morning since she could remember. She was glad that her father hadn't been pressed into military service like those of her close friends. His engineering skills, which were very valuable to the South Vietnamese Government, had kept him from being inducted into the Army. Although her family owned a small apartment in the heart of My Tho, she was grateful to the government that her family was allowed to live in the warehouses, which housed material used by the engineering commands. It was part of her father's job to oversee the distribution of these supplies; this was the reason that he had to turn in his reports every Saturday morning to the province chief.

She glanced outside and noticed her mother stirring noodles in the large cooking pot. She swatted at the two youngest kids with the wooden ladle as she caught them trying to fish the long rice noodles out of the pot with their hands. The strong, sweet smell of incense stung her nostrils as her younger brother passed her and stuck the long, simmering stems into the small bowl of uncooked rice set on the bamboo shelf. Grateful that her mother had let her sleep late, she rolled up the nylon woven sleeping mat and folded up the sides of the mosquito netting. She was suddenly apprehensive. Today was Saturday, the day that her father was to meet her beloved Gary. The tall, gentle American had added a new meaning to her life. She turned to the burning incense and breathed a silent prayer to the Father Buddha.

All of her brothers and sisters had gathered around the table, patiently waiting for their morning breakfast of noodle soup. She walked over to the cupboard and, took out ten soup bowls, and placed them in front of each of the children. In the olden days, a family was considered blessed if it was this large, but now it was a hardship, she thought to herself as she spooned out the noodles into each bowl.

She was thankful to Buddha that her family had as much as they did, she thought, as she picked up a piece of thinly sliced pork and dropped it into each of the bowls. At least now, their family could afford to buy meat since she had started working for the Americans. If Gary really had the intention of marrying her, as she hoped, then she could really help her family. Her mother liked the tall American, whom she said was too respectful to be an American. She had also told her that she had inherited affairs of the heart from her, referring to the peculiar story of their meeting.

Her mother was of noble birth, while her father had been a common criminal who had raided her mother's caravan and held her captive. He had buried her up to her neck in the sand until her mother had promised to marry him. The two of them had fallen deeply in love by the time her grandfather's troops had cornered the outlaws between the Laotian and Vietnamese border and captured them. Her mother had begged her grandfather for her father's life, which he consented to, sparing him as long as she and her criminal husband left the country, never to return. Her mother and father had fled south to Hue City, where she had been born. She had one brother and three sisters by the time she was seven years old. Her father had taken some of the gold that he had stolen during his career as a criminal and invested it in a Chinese restaurant. Within five years, he had made a small fortune catering food to the French Army. He then sold the restaurant when she was ten years old and moved the family south to Saigon. Her family had arrived in Saigon with all their family fortune inside a large suitcase.

She knew the story well, as to how her mother had left the suitcase unattended while she was eating lunch. A Saigon slicky boy had grabbed the suitcase and made off with it. Her father still blamed her mother to this day for the misery that her family had suffered after that. One good thing had come from the incident: her father had sought work digging ditches for the French engineers. He had been taken under the tutorship of one of the French engineers, who taught him the French language and basic engineering skills.

"Hurry up and eat; you all have to hurry off to school," she said with a sigh as she sat down on one of the empty stools.

"Do American children go to school?" asked Be the, the next eldest girl in the family.

"Silly kid, every child in every country has to go to school if their family can afford it," she replied.

"Why do I have to go to school? I'm old enough to go to work for the Americans and make money like you do," she retorted.

"Yes, me too; I can sell candy and cokes," volunteered Cong Rum, the second eldest son.

"All of you stop talking nonsense and get up and go to school," she scolded them sternly.

Things quieted down after the six kids got their book packs and left for school. She wondered how her father was able to send all her brothers and sisters to school. Although they went to a Buddhist religious school, he still had to pay a lot of money to send them. Thang, the oldest boy, would be graduating this year. He had already made a high enough score on his civil service test, which would allow him to attend the military academy next spring. She didn't see the need to send all her sisters to school, but her father was very stern when it came to education and demanded the best from each child. It was after midnight many nights before the children finished their studies.

She walked outside to see if she could help her mother with the chores.

The bellowing smoke and noisy engine of one of the American Army vehicles brought her mind back to Gary as she watched it bounce across the wooden bridge in front of her house. He had asked her and her mother and father out to dinner that evening. She hadn't mentioned the brown-haired American to her father. She just knew he would be furious when Gary asked him for her hand in marriage, as he had told her he planned to do.

I guess now is as good a time as any, she thought to herself as she walked up to her mother.

"Mother, what do you think Father will say if Gary asks him for me this afternoon?" she asked worriedly.

"There's one thing I want to ask you," her mother said. "I know that you are a very obedient daughter, and I trust you to the fullest, but I need to know—has the American made love to you yet?"

"No, Mother, he hasn't even tried. I love him so much that I couldn't resist him if he tried, but he hasn't. He treats me with the utmost respect."

"Then that's all I need to know. You just leave your father to me. I'll handle him."

"Thanks, Mother," she said as she hugged her and kissed her forehead softly. "You'll never be sorry, I promise you."

"I'll leave that up to you. What time is he coming?"

"He said that he would be here at three o'clock."

"Then you had better take a bath and make yourself beautiful. You don't want to disappoint him."

"Mom, you are the best," she said, giving her another kiss and a hug.

"I made a promise to Buddha before you were born that if I ever had a girl child, I would never stand in the way of her happiness. Also, I like the big American and think he would make a good father for my grandchildren. Now hurry and get ready; your father will be back shortly. I'll go and make arrangements for a taxi to come and pick us up."

She heard the squeaking brakes of her father's bicycle as he coasted to a stop outside the entrance to the warehouse. Although her father was very stern at times, he was a kind and loving father who always took care of his family. The first thing she planned to do after she was married was buy him a Japanese motorcycle. She might even be able to buy a French villa. Americans were so rich, and if Gary really loved her as much as he seemed to, it wouldn't be too hard to convince him, she thought as she buttoned the side of her dress. She would also buy her mother some beautiful dresses. It felt good to be in love, especially with a rich American.

She glanced at the old wind-up clock that sat on top of her parents' chest, which stored the few good clothes the family had. This had been a good year for her family. The whole family had been able to buy a new set of clothes this last New Year's holiday. It was customary to buy at least one set of clothes every New Year to bring health and prosperity to the family. It was nearly two-thirty. She had to get her father ready before Gary showed up. She didn't want to cause her future husband...

She became anxious, having to wait for her mother and father. She also had to issue instructions to the little ones, warning them not to act like little heathens. At first, the little ones had been shy and afraid of the big American, but now, because of his spoiling them with kindness, they had become little nuisances. Every time he showed up, they surrounded him, demanding tributes. He seemed pleased that they had taken up with him, but they worried her a lot, begging candy from him like little street urchins. She knew that she must be stern with him and ask him to stop giving them candy. She knew if her father saw them, he would become very angry with her.

She was awakened from her random thoughts by the screaming of the little ones.

"He's coming! He's coming! The American is coming. Hurry, let's go see if he has brought us any candy!"

"You kids stay inside the house and stop running out in the road! If you don't stop begging the American for candy, I am going to tell Father," she scolded them sternly.

She heard the scuffing of his heavy Army boots on the gravel roadside that led into their dwelling.

"Thanh!" she called out to her younger brother. "Show Gary into the front room and introduce him to Father. Tell him that I will be out as soon as I finish dressing."

As her younger brother rushed out to intercept the American, she left the door slightly cracked to observe the meeting between the American and her father. Her father was sitting cross-legged on the wide platform that served as a couch, eating table, and bed for her father and four brothers as her younger brother ushered the American in and introduced him to her father, who looked up from his paper and said something that she could not quite hear. She closely studied the features of her father's face for any sign of disapproval as she watched her younger brother set the package down in front of her father.

She watched as the American stepped up to the platform on which her father was sitting. Her father again spoke to her brother, nodding at the package that was sitting beside him. She watched as the taller American saluted her father in the customary fashion of the Vietnamese people. She breathed a sigh of relief as a broad grin crossed her father's face. Now was the time for her to make her entrance, she thought, as she finished buttoning the collar of her Ao Dia.

"Looks like you have already met my father," she said as she walked into the area that served as a small restaurant during the day and sleeping quarters at night. "How are the two of you getting along?"

"We have a slight language barrier that we have to work out. Besides that, we are hitting it off quite well. I have been trying to explain to your father that I have brought him a few gifts. Would you explain it to him for me?" the American asked in reply.

She picked up the package and handed it to her father. "Father, this is for you. Please open it up."

Taking the package from her hand, her father opened it up and took out a bottle of Johnny Walker and several cartons of Salem cigarettes.

"Bring us two glasses, and we'll have a drink," he instructed her as he picked up the bottle and prepared to twist the cap off.

"NO! NO! Don't open up the bottle because of me," the American said, grabbing her father's hand and stopping him from breaking the seal of the bottle. "Tell your father that I don't drink or smoke and that he needn't open up the whiskey on my account."

"Father, don't open any of those gifts. My friend doesn't drink or smoke. Later, mother will take the gifts and sell them on the black market. They will bring as much as one month of my wages," she informed her father.

"Then fix some cokes for us to drink," her father

beckoned her as he pulled the big American to a sitting position on the edge of the platform.

That was a comical picture, two of them made, she thought, as she went to the cupboard and took out two of her mother's best glasses. The huge American made her father look like a dwarf. She must go out and hasten her mother; the taxi would be here at any time, she thought, as she poured coke over the ice in the two glasses. In the meantime, she had to get Gary away from her father long enough to talk with him privately. After she had set the cokes down in front of her father, she excused herself and walked out to where her mother was preparing the kids' evening meal.

"Mother, you go in and get ready to go. I will finish cooking the meal for the children," she said, taking the wooden ladle from her hand.

"Ok," her mother agreed, stating that Bae Te, her younger sister of four years, could serve the food to the children after they came home from school.

Her mother looked so old and tired, she thought, as she watched her hurry into the warehouse. After she had married, she planned to hire a housemaid and cook to help her mother.

"Gary! Gary!" she called out. "Would you come out here? I need to talk to you."

She watched through the open window as the American got up and excused himself from her father, and walked outside to the cookhouse.

"What do you think of my father?" she asked.

"It's not so important what I think of him; my worry is whether or not he will accept me," he replied.

"My father, he likes you, I know. I saw his face when he met you for the first time. Do you see how big he smiled?" she stated in broken English.

"I hope so. I love you so much. It would make me very unhappy if your father were against me from the start. What do you think he will say when we ask for his blessing to be married?" the American asked her worriedly.

"Don't worry. If he doesn't like me, my mother will change his mind. I already spoke to my mother about you asking me to marry. She's very happy. She says not to worry; she will handle my father. One thing, please try to eat a little of the food at the restaurant. If my father knows you eat Vietnamese food, he will like you more."

"That's not a problem. I like Vietnamese food. It's very tasty," he replied.

"Good! One thing that no worry me, I finished cooking my brother and sister's food. Oh! Here comes the taxi," she exclaimed, pointing to an oncoming vehicle approaching the rickety bridge a short distance from her house. "Hurry, we must go see if my mother is ready to go."

Thui had everyone assembled by the edge of the gravel road just as the taxi pulled to a stop in front of the warehouse. After seeing that an American was with them, the driver asked for three times the fare that she had arranged. This angered her father, who refused to get into the taxi and was ready to send the taxi away without a fare.

"What's happening?" asked the American after noting that no one was getting into the taxi.

"The driver has raised the fare three times the amount he first agreed. He says you are too big, you break his taxi," she explained.

The big American gave a good-natured laugh. "Tell the driver that I will pay him three thousand won if he will let us hire him for the rest of the evening."

"That's too much money. The driver doesn't make that much money in one week," she replied.

"Today is a special day; the money is not important. Ask the driver if he will agree."

"Okay, but only if you don't think it's too much money," she said, turning back to the taxi driver.

"The American wants me to ask if we can hire the car for the rest of the evening," she inquired.

"Sure, it will cost two thousand won," the driver answered in reply.

Feeling quite satisfied with her bargaining, she gave the taxi driver directions to the restaurant. Noticing a roadside food stand adjacent to the restaurant, she ordered him his dinner, paying for it in advance.

"Wait here and eat. After a couple of hours, I will need you to drive my mother and father back to our home," she instructed the driver.

The owners of the restaurant were the family of one of her high school friends. Many times, after school had been let out, she had come home with her to help in the restaurant. Her friend had married a soldier and moved to Dai Lac, leaving her at a loss. They very seldom had the chance to visit each other.

Her friend's mother met her at the entrance to the restaurant. Two days ago, she had sent a note from her younger brother Thang, leaving instructions for the engagement party.

"What's the special occasion?" her friend's mother asked, eyeing the American suspiciously. "I know it isn't your nor your parents' birthday. What's that American doing coming here with all of you? Is he your boss or something?"

"Please have patience, Aunt. You will find out all in good time," she replied with a laugh.

"Please follow me. I have a table set up in the rear of the restaurant like you asked," said her friend's mother, leading the party to the rear of the restaurant.

"Father, you sit here," she instructed, pulling out a chair at the head of the table. "Gary can sit next to me. Mother, you sit on the other side."

"Is that the American's name? Does he have any other or only one name? I will have a hard time pronouncing his name. I think I'll just continue calling him Mr. American like the young ones do," her father said.

"All of you will have to learn to pronounce his name. Mother has already learned his name. No, Father, most all Americans have three names, as do Vietnamese. His full name is Gary Wayne Gray, Gray being his surname as Vo is ours."

"What are you talking about?" the American asked after hearing his name mentioned.

"My father wants to know what all of your names are," she explained. " he says that he thinks he will have trouble remembering how to pronounce your name," she replied.

"What's your father's full name?" the American asked.

"Vo Van Hoan, but you must call him Ba, which means father, and call my mother Ma," she replied. " here comes the food. After it is served, you can make the announcement of our marriage engagement."

"What's all this food for? I thought that we were only having a small party. There's enough food here for a party of twenty. What is going on anyway?" her father asked suspiciously.

"Gary is going to explain now. He has an announcement to make," she answered.

Reaching under the table, she caught the American's hand and squeezed it. "Now you can tell my parents of our plans to get married," she said, giving his hand another loving squeeze.

"Okay, I'll speak and you translate for me. If they have any questions, you stop me, and I'll answer the best I can."

Sitting up taller in his chair, he cleared his throat nervously. "Ba, Ma," he started, using the Vietnamese version of mother and father. "Thui and I have known each other for six months. During this time, I have grown to love her very much and wish you to give us permission to marry."

Closely, she studied her father's face as she translated the message. He remained calm as he was noted for, still showing no sign of emotion.

"I have applied and been approved for a six-month extension to my tour here in Vietnam. This will give us eight months to process all the paperwork."

She again translated to her father and mother.

"What will you do if I don't give you my approval?" her father asked.

"I will move out and live by ourselves anyway. I don't want to lose him," she replied. "Father, I love Gary more than..."

"Have you made love to him?" her mother asked.

"No, mother, but I would if he insisted. He is a very honorable man. He has never insisted on making love. He also said that he was willing to wait until we are married."

"Ask him what he will do if I don't give the two of you permission to marry or if the paperwork takes longer than eight months to finish," her father instructed her.

"Tell him that my heart would be broken if he didn't permit us and that I wouldn't go against his wishes. As for the paperwork, I will remain in Vietnam as long as it is necessary," the American told her to inform her father.

"Indeed, he seems to be an honorable man," her father said after she had again translated. "Tell him that you are my eldest daughter and that your mother and I both would hate to lose you to America. We may never see you again, nor our grandchildren, but if you are happy and he will give his word to take care of you, we give the two of you our blessings."

Upon hearing this, she sprang up from the table and threw her arms around her father's neck, giving him a big hug, tears of joy filling her eyes.

"From your reaction, I take it that they have given us their approval," the American said, standing up. He bent over and kissed her mother on the cheek, and hugged her father from the other side. "Tell your father that he has made me the happiest man in Vietnam," he said.

"Mrs. Min, bring us bottles of beer. We are going to celebrate our daughter's engagement to marry," her father called out to the waitress.

"You have to drink a little with my father. He wants to celebrate," she told the American.

"Tell your father that I am ready to celebrate this occasion. Your mother is wearing the most beautiful necklace that I have ever seen. Where did she buy it? I would like to buy one like it for a wedding present."

"It's made from imperial jade. It's very valuable. It was given to my mother by her mother. When I marry, it will be passed on down to me. It has been in our family for many generations," she replied.

"Tell your mother that it enhances her beauty, makes her look like a queen," the American said, raising his glass up to toast the engagement party.

"To our life together."

****

Chapter 6

There was a time when it seemed to me that Vietnam had forgotten that there was a war. In December of 1969, everything was quiet around Dong Tam. The Viet Cong slowed the mortaring of the compound to about one or two per week. Nothing seemed to slow the preparation for Tet, the Vietnamese New Year. The upcoming event was to occur around February 6, 1970. The sweet fragrance of brightly colored flowers mingled with the sweet aroma of all kinds of exotic fruits, which were piled high in all the marketplaces.

The sweet smells of flowers and fruits suppressed the pungent stench of the rice paddies. Tailors were extra busy sewing new clothes for families to adorn during the Tet season holidays. New clothes were a must to bring good luck for the upcoming year.

The military was making preparations of its own. During Tet of 1968, the military was caught completely off guard. The Viet Cong entered and ransacked My Tho, leaving the city full of dead Vietnamese officials and civilian employees who worked on military installations. The commanding general of IV Corps set a curfew of 18 hours on all military traffic traveling the roadways throughout the region. All entertainment establishments in the cities and villages across the IV Corps area were put on a restricted list. All company commanders were instructed to enforce strict accountability of all American military personnel.

Military police patrolled the roads and streets and arrested anyone they caught out on the streets. This being the case, any of us who had girlfriends and wives were forced to slip out from the compound after dark. This was a dangerous endeavor. We could have been mistaken for Viet Cong and shot by perimeter guards. During the first few weeks in December, I caught rides into My Tho with military vehicles going to Camp Viking.

The base was adjacent to the small runway on which I first landed upon my arrival in the delta. Thui's home was located directly across from the front gate. Most times, it was easy to catch a ride back to the barracks with vehicles returning to base for the evening. Most soldiers leaving the base were required to return to the base before 1800 hours. At other times, it was difficult to catch a ride back to Dong Tam. On these occasions, I was forced to hire a three-wheeled taxi to drive me within one-half mile of the front gates. One evening, a week before Christmas in 1970, after not finding a ride, I decided to walk the five-mile distance back to the barracks.

It was after 2200 hours when I left Thui's home and commenced the 40-minute walk. I should have pondered the oddity of the lack of taxis around on that evening. It was quite dark walking down the road. Thick banana plants covered the sides of the road. Tall bamboo trees on each side of the road cast shadows that met in the middle of the road. The trees were tall and leafy, making the shadows dance about as the breeze gently swayed them. After twenty or so minutes of walking, I noticed the flicker of a cigarette lighter coming from the shadows about 100 yards ahead of me. I stopped walking and, slipped into the shadows of the bamboo plants and waited. A moonlight ray shone through a break in the vegetation, casting a 20-foot wide strip across the road. The moonlight ray ran across the road at the spot where I had seen the cigarette lighter flicker. After waiting for a few minutes, I saw a formation of troops dart across the road in the moonlight. I noticed the uniforms were dark and did not seem right. A little frightened, I turned and hastily walked back down the road, trying to stay in the shadows.

After I had walked back about two hundred yards, I stopped again. I noticed the headlights of vehicles coming towards me. I slipped into the shadows once more, anticipating the need to hide in case it was an MP patrol "Duck"(the name given to armored personnel carriers used by the Military Police). I waited until the headlights drew closer and then noticed that it was a military jeep. I also noticed two Duce-and-Half (two-ton utility trucks) following the jeep. I turned my flashlight on and waved it from side to side, signaling for the convoy to stop. The jeep pulled to a stop beside me. I noticed a Vietnamese captain riding in the passenger seat.

"Tại sao bạn lại ngăn cản tôi," he asked? (Asking why I had stopped the convoy)

"Tôi thấy vài người lính mặc áo đen băng qua đường phía trước khoảng một trăm mét,"I replied in broken Vietnamese. (I saw a military formation wearing dark black uniforms cross the road about one hundred yards ahead)

"You speak good Vietnamese," he replied in fluent English. I again told him in English about seeing individuals who looked like troops dressed in black pajamas dart across the road ahead of us. He quickly informed me that there were no VRF troops (Vietnamese Reserve Forces) in the area. He said they were most likely the Viet Cong, setting up to ambush a passing convoy. He ordered his first sergeant to tell the troops to disembark the vehicles and make a tactical sweep along the roadside. About twenty or thirty troops got out of the vehicles and slipped out of sight into the roadside's shadows. After I stood waiting beside the jeep for about fifteen minutes, all hell broke loose. Suddenly, a firefight burst out about two hundred feet ahead of us that lasted about 30 minutes.

Shortly after that, the troops came back down the road to return to the vehicles. They were marching three individuals ahead of the formation, dressed in black pajamas. The fellows' hands were tied behind their backs, and they were blindfolded. They were grabbed roughly by a couple of troops and thrown into the back of the first Duce-and-Half. The Vietnamese captain informed me that his troops had killed six more VC and left the bodies lying beside the road. He said it was a warning to other VCs in the area.

He asked me where I was going. I told him that I had just left my Vietnamese wife's home and was walking back to Dong Tam.

"You couldn't find a Lamberti Taxi?" he asked.

"No, there were none around this evening, as there usually are," I answered.

"That's because villagers in this area seem to know when the Viet Cong are engaging in operations nearby. If this happens in the future, you should return home and wait until the next day," he informed me.

"Could I get a ride with you back to Dong Tam?"I asked.

"For sure, that's the least we can do for you. You're stopping us, most likely, saved lives by not letting us ride into an ambush," he replied.

I rode the rest of the way into Dong Tam with the convoy. I was also lucky the convoy had come by and gave me a ride. The base was on top alert and was checking everyone who drove through.

"What are you doing with these guys?" asked one of the sergeants guarding the front gate.

"I am this platoon's MACV advisor. We just drove through an ambush between here and My Tho. There was a firefight down the road. These troops killed six VCs and captured three. We are taking the three they captured to the prison compound on base," I answered.

"Yeah, I heard the commotion and wondered what it was about. Sir, you guys have a good evening," he said as he waved us through the gate.

We continued with the prisoners to the stockade located in the center of Dong Tam. The stockade was constructed by engineers to hold NVA troops (North Vietnamese Army) and Viet Cong sympathizers captured by the 9th Infantry. The stockade was about two blocks from my barracks.

"Làm thế nào để bạn nói lời cảm ơn cho chuyến đi?"I said to the ARVN captain as I exited the jeep. (Thank you for giving me the ride here.)

The support airfields in South Vietnam were typically 3,500 feet long and 60 feet wide. The runways were also required to have a paved area that could accommodate three C-130 aircraft. The Air Force had strict specifications as to how support runways were to be constructed, and these needed to be met before the aircraft were allowed to land.

The 93rd Engineers built protective berms 6 to 10 feet high along the sides of Dong Tam runway. These berms were used to protect ammunition and fuel storage areas during Viet Cong attacks. During World War II and the Korean War, most runway surfacing was constructed of PSP, large steel planks with punched holes. Large stocks of this material were in South Vietnam long before troops arrived. It was widely used for lining truck beds and the floors of other transportation vehicles. PSP was not much help in covering large holes. Mud seeped through the holes in the expanded metal, causing it to sink down to water level.

It was a great relief to the South Vietnamese and the engineers when M8A1, solid steel aluminum planking, arrived. Company C, 93rd Engineers, was tasked to repair and extend the runway at Dong Tam. Dong Tam was located on the right bank of the My Tho River, a tributary flowing from the My Cong River. After completion, the runway would run from the edge of the bank north towards Saigon. The Brown Water Navy had a small base at the edge of the river, and the extended runway would expand the base. Company C was assigned to the project, and my task was to operate a 290M Earthmover.

We emptied bags of cement and sand into the five-yard scoop of a front-end loader. After the scoop was full, the mixture of sand and cement was emptied into the scraper of the 290M Earthmover. The scraper held four loads of the mixture, approximately twenty yards. The scraper was used to spread the mixture over the prepared runway surface. Approximately 8 inches of the concrete and sand mixture were spread over a surface area, which was then rolled and compacted with a steel drum roller. After the surface was compacted, it was moisturized with a water tanker truck's sprayer attachment.

After a 3,000-square-foot section of the runway was completed, the area was covered with a rubber membrane. The membrane came in 100 x 60-yard rolls, which were easy to use and quick to install. The rubber also provided a durable, waterproof, dustproof surface that retained moisture until the cement dried. Each roll cost $1,000. Once the membrane had served its purpose, it was removed, piled high, and set afire. The fire bellowed black smoke that covered the entire base camp. A lot of money was burned in those piles since it took close to one hundred rolls to cover the runway. However, it did serve its purpose by maintaining Air Force construction standards.

It was a hard, hot, dirty job. The cement often burned the skin when the bags were ripped open. Troops with black skin suffered the worse. I often notice the flesh burn away in patches to reveal white skin below. The Viet Cong often mortared us. We got so familiar with the harassment that we could hear the pop of the motor rounds being fired from the jungle. The pop sound warned us it was time to hit one of the nearest bunkers we had constructed along the runway. One afternoon, a mortar struck the runway 50 yards close to where we were working.

The unexploded round cut us off from the closest bunker. We cautiously and slowly walked fifty yards and then high-tailed it to the nearest bunker. That stopped our work on the runway until the EOD team came and exploded the round in place.

When we were not doing construction work on the runway, we took over the 9th Infantry's perimeter security duties. My platoon's position was on the west end of the base along the My Tho River. This position was easy to defend. Most of the troops sat in the bunkers and smoked dope all night. Since I didn't drink or smoke dope, I spent many boring and lonely nights sitting in guard towers. It finally reached the point that I hated dope smokers. They did dangerous things with the equipment, and those of us who didn't smoke dope had to take up the slack they caused. There were numerous industrial accidents related to loading and unloading heavy equipment from lowboy trailers. These accidents occurred due to troops being drunk or stoned on dope. One Eighteen-Wheeler driver in Company B had more accidents than anyone else. He had "**Widow Maker Stenciled**" across the hood of his ten-ton tractor; later, the next year, his prophecy was fulfilled.

I was tying to learn the Vietnamese and often engaged the hooch maids to teach me. One day, my Platoon Lieutenant overheard me talking to one of the Vietnamese housemaids. He stopped and asked me if I really wanted to learn to speak Vietnamese. I told him that it was a great desire of mine, especially now, since I had a Vietnamese girlfriend and was determined to marry her and take her back to America. He offered to order a Vietnamese Language Coorspondance course from the Monterey School of Language. I asked him to please order one for me.

He ordered the Correspondence course and it arrived about a month later. The Correspondence course opens an opportunity for me to learn to read, speak, and write fluent Vietnamese within six months. The most difficult was learning to pronounce the accents above the words, for example, the words (ma = ghost) (má = mother) mà = but) (mả = tomb) (mã = horse) (mạ = rice seedling). The lieutenant and I became close friends. He chose me to drive his jeep and interpret for him during his tour. He achieved B Company Commander before his Deros in 1971. Making friends with the Lieutenant was a lucky break for me and Thui. We were required to have permission from my company commander before the military would recognize our marriage. He gave us the letter of permission before he left. I will always be grateful to him. If he is reading this book, he will know I am mentioning him.

Thui and I were very busy planning our wedding. We made plans to get married close to my in-country anniversary in May 1971. I had finally made E-5 and was drawing $408 each month. We saved most of mymilitary pay and made extra money engaging in Black market activities. Together, we had accumulated close to ten thousand dollars. The first task was getting our fortune read by a fortune reader. The office was on the outskirts of My Tho, near the bus terminal. The fortune reader was a gentleman dressed in a neatly pressed suit. He asked each of us about our birthday dates. He looked at Thui's palm first and told her something that was hard for me to understand. He followed the lines on the palm of her hand with his right forefinger.

He would mumble something under his breath and keep repeating the process. After about 20 minutes he let go of her hand and went through the same process with me. He didn't spend as much time reading my palm. I wondered if it was because my hand was much bigger and easier to read or if I had a shorter lifespan. I was a little worried. She gave me a synopsis of the reading after we exited his office. The fortune teller told her that our signs were compatible.

That we would have one son and two daughters, and he said that all our children would make us very proud in our old age. Thui further confided to me that the fortune teller had told her that I had an odd aura that closely resembled an Asian aura. He told her my aura was different than most American palms he had read. I thought about it for a few minutes; then the answer came to me. I realized in my what he could have seen in my aura. I told her that my maternal grandmother was fifty percent Indian; maybe that is what he noticed. Suddenly, a look of sadness and fear flashed across her face; her eyes widened, she raised her eyebrows, and her mouth opened slightly.

"What's wrong?"I asked after seeing the look on her face.

"Oh, it's nothing; I was thinking about something else he told me," she replied.

"Gosh! I hope it's not as bad as you think," I answered back. "Everything will all work out."Let's go back home.

I never thought much of the incident after that. We returned to Thui's home. She informed her parents that the fortune teller picked June 1 as the best day for our wedding. Thui and her mother set a the kitchen table and started a guest list. She had an aunt who lived in Tan An. A small city in the Long An Province located between My Tho and Saigon. She planned where to have the venue in the recreation at center of the ARVN compound (the name of the Vietnamese Army base). The Base Recreation Center had a small restaurant and lounge. The restaurant is large enough to hold 200 guests. We were planning to invite a few buddies. My Commanding Officer and a few friends from the RMK-BRJ construction company. I had become close friends with a couple of RMK-BRJ diesel truck mechanics. We chose the ARVN compound due to the security it provided. The last thing task they had was to choose Thui's áo dài, her Vietnamese wedding dress. She would need four of them during the ceremony.

"Tạm biệt mẹ, Tôi phải trở về doanh trại quân đội, I said to Thui's mother. (Mother, I have to return to the Barracks, I will return next Saturday)

"Hãy quay lại nhanh nhé, chúng tôi nhớ bạn," (Hurry back, we will miss you) She answered with a big smile on her face. She liked for me to try to use Vietnamese.

"Cô Thui anh yêu em, thứ bảy tuần sau anh sẽ về., (Miss Thui, I love only you forever and ever) I told Thui and exited the front door. Thui followed me only to the door, did not go outside with me and gave me a hearted kiss.

"Me Too," she replied as she closed the front door.

I returned to the barracks happy and in good spirits. Thui had told me that the wedding would cost us over $7000 in MPC. I knew that we had saved over 100,000 won, equivalent to 10,000 dollars. I hope that it would be sufficient Thui's mother estimated we would need to buy one cow to butcher, six piglets, 100 ducks, and 100 chickens. I remember once a dump truck hit a cow and killed it.

The incident cost the driver five hundred dollars in MPC. I estimated a piglet would cost at least $50 each; add another $300 for 100 ducks and 100 chickens. I had managed to purchase and put aside 40 cases of Budweiser Beer. I had purchased a pallet of beer from a friend who ran the Dong Tam NCO club for three dollars a case. I was not planning to serve hard liquor. Most of the younger GIs and the ARVN troops could not handle hard liquor. The reception will be held in the ARVN Compound Recreation Center. My estimation of the cost of the reception was close to $1500 just for the meat products. After paying for the preparation of the food, the use of the Rec Center and cases of 33 beer, all-in-all, the reception would cost close to 5000 dollars.

Monday morning, I went to work as usual. We had completed the Runway project and were moving on to larger projects. The 20th Engineer Brigade was tasked with building bridges and roads across the delta and the central highlands of Vietnam. The 93rd battalion was assigned a large section of the My Cong delta. Company 93rd was tasked to build a road from My Tho towards the south to Ben Tre. A section was completed from My Tho to Binh Phu. To complete the project to Ben Tre we had to cross one of the My Cong tributaries.

The river was approximately two hundred yards across. The only way to cross was on a floating Baliey bridge. We had set up a Ferry system to move vehicles to and fro across the river. This was accomplished by attaching a 5/8 inch round steel cable, 300 feet long, to each end of the bridge. The ends of the cables were then attached to the hitch of a 290M Tactor located on each side of the river. One tractor would pull while the other backed, keeping the cables tight and the floating bridge straight.

On this particular Monday, I was assigned to be the platoon sergeant's driver to drive him to the job site. We left DongTam directly after morning chow and drove the one-hour trip to the jobsite. I had just bought a small portable radio a couple of weeks prior, listening to it while I drove around. I hung the radio in the open rear window of the truck.

The rear window of the ¾ ton M880 truck is a patch of clear plastic attached to a large strip of canvas. The canvas is easily rolled up and secured to the top of the truck cab. The street was heavily congested with of people, bicycles, vehicles, and street vendors. I had the volume on the radio turned up loud to be able to hear the music. The volume of the music on the radio decreased as I drove slowly down the street. All of a sudden, the music faded from my hearing.

"Hey, sarge, turn the volume on the radio back up," I requested.

"What radio! It's not there!" he answered as he turned in his seat to do so.

"Man, those kids are really good little thieves. They can cop a radio while we are listening to it," I replied.

"Beats the hell out of me. Don't know how they do it," he replied.

"They must be grabbing it and walking away while turning the volume down as they walk," I offered.

We both checked to see if our M16s were still in their mounting racks. Breathing a sigh of relief, we continued to the job site. We camped out at the job site for the rest of that week. Billeting at s MACV compound located in the area. We drove back to Dong Tam late Friday night. The platoon sergeant had to attend a staff meeting where the CO would discuss issues that arose during the week. When we reached My Tho on the return trip, I asked if I could stop off and check on my fiancée. He permitted me and said he would cover for me and to be back at the barracks by 1800 hours on Sunday. I walked the short distance to Thui's home from the spot he dropped me off.

When I walked through the front door, I sensed something was wrong. For one thing, the kids did not run to me and start searching my pockets. Thui's father walked on from the rear of the building, not looking so happy. He told me that Thui was gone, and he could not find her. He told me he had traveled to every place that he thought she could have gone. He couldn't find her. It was late in the afternoon and too late to go looking for her. I told him to get some sleep, and that I would start looking in the morning.

****

Chapter 7

Thui unzipped the mosquito netting, making an opening in the middle. Slowly, she slipped through, trying not to awaken her three younger sisters, who were sleeping soundly on the knee-high platform. She had informed her mother the previous evening that she was going to the market early. She could hear her mother moving about in the adjacent bedroom shared by her parents and her eight- month-old baby brother.

As the eldest child with eleven younger siblings, their ages ranged from eight months to sixteen years. Four of her siblings were boys, and three were girls. Her younger sisters were four, six, and eight years old. All the children attended a Confucius school approximately three miles away from their home. The children would wake up soon to get ready for the walk to school. Thui provided most of the care for her siblings and had done so for the majority of her young life. She had once mentioned this responsibility to Gary, who had told her not to worry. He assured her that all her responsibilities would become his once they were married, promising that her family was his family and they would do whatever it took to make everything work. She loved Gary so very much and believed he would make a perfect husband. He let her manage all the money and trusted her with spending it wisely.

However, Thui had grown concerned about the feasibility of their marriage after learning from a fortune reader that Gary's ancestry contained Asian blood. He had told her that his grandmother was fifty percent Indian, and now she knew their marriage would never work.

It had been difficult enough convincing her parents to permit her to marry an American, but now she would have to inform them that Gary's maternal grandmother was half-Indian. They would never approve. Girls from good families did not choose husbands or wives from India. It was contrary to Vietnamese culture and norms for the two cultures to intermingle.

She had made the decision yesterday to run away after Gary had gone back to the barracks. She would stay gone until he returned to America. Thui reached under the edge of the platform and pulled out a small suitcase, which she had packed with a few clothes, pictures, and other personal items the previous evening. Grasping the handle, she walked a short distance down the gravel road, walking away from the ARVN Military compound where her family lived. Her father was employed as a civil servant for the Republic of Vietnam, in charge of purchasing and issuing building supplies for Vietnamese military specialists and civil engineers.

When she reached the paved street coming from Dong Tam and passing through My Tho, she stopped a rickshaw and engaged the operator to take her to the bus stop on the outskirts of My Tho. She bought a one-way ticket to Saigon, boarded the bus, and sat in the vacant seat behind the driver. She tapped him on the shoulder and asked him to stop and let her off in Cho Lon. Cho Lon was on the outskirts of Saigon, in an area where all the rich Chinese lived. Thui had a high school girlfriend who lived with and worked for one of the wealthy Chinese families in the city. She hoped her friend might help her find a job with another rich Chinese family in the area.

After about a thirty-minute ride, with numerous stops to pick up and drop off passengers, she finally reached Cho Lon. She hired another rickshaw to take her to the address her friend had previously provided. Thui spent the day visiting with her friend and the lady of the house. In the afternoon, her friend's boss took her to another Chinese family's home, a close friend of theirs. The woman hired

Thui right away on the recommendation of her friend's boss. She made a deal to work as a housemaid for the family, receiving room and board plus 50,000 Wong per month.

Thui worked hard throughout the week, getting the family's younger children ready for school and washing clothes every day. She was very unhappy and depressed, going to bed late every night. She wept quietly until she fell asleep, beginning to think she had made a wrong decision. She desperately wanted to return home but was too afraid. Her father had never beaten her, but she wondered if he might after the stunt she had pulled. She wished desperately that Gary would find her and take her back home, though there was no way he could ever find her. Her parents must be worried sick, not knowing where she was or how to find her.

She awoke on Saturday morning, which felt like the hardest yet. Saturdays were the days Gary would come. What would he think of her when he found out she had run away from home? He must be extremely angry and think she was a very deceitful person. She started her morning chores and prepared to do her daily washing. She much preferred doing the washing for her own family, she thought, as she filled the large plastic tub with water.

The same Saturday morning, I awoke early and went to the bus station. I had deduced that if I showed Thui's picture to all the bus drivers, someone might remember her. There was a small restaurant with a few tables where passengers and bus drivers sometimes sat and drank tea while waiting for a bus. It was the start of one of my most lucky days. As I walked into the restaurant, I bumped into an operator just coming back out. I showed him Thui's picture and asked him if he remembered her.

He told me that he surely did. The last Monday, she got on his bus and sat in the seat behind the driver's seat. He said she seemed to have been crying and would not talk much. He said she got off the bus when he stopped at the Cho Lon bus stop. I told him that I wanted to go to

Cho Lon to, where she got off the bus. He told me that he was starting the route now and that I should buy a ticket and come with him. We walked to the bus together, and I got on and sat down in a vacant seat near him.

After about forty minutes, we arrived at Cho Lon City. He stopped the bus and told me that this was the spot where she got off. Cho Lon is on the outskirts of Saigon. A small river separates the two cities. The city was founded in 1778 by Chinese emigrants. The two cities are unified commercially and physically by streetcars, roads, and canals. The city was not as damaged during the war as other cities within the region. Some believed it was due to the Chinese relationship with Communist China. Most of the citizens were rich Chinese. After I exited the bus, I walked over to an area that held 10 or 12 rickshaws. I began to show Thui's photo to the operators.

After four or five drivers viewed the photo, finally, one of them finally recognized her. He told me that he had taken her to a house not too far away. I asked if I could hire him to take me to the home. When we arrived, I asked him to wait for me while I checked if she was there. He agreed, and we left to make the trip. He stopped in front of a huge Chinese mansion with a wrought iron gate in front. I went to the gate and rang a brass bell. A young Vietnamese maiden came to the gate and opened it up.

"Anh có phải là bạn của em không, chồng Thui?" she inquired with a startled look. (Are you my friend Thui's husband?)

"Vâng, tôi đang tìm Thui,"I replied. (Yes, I am looking for her.) "Đợi ở đây, tôi sẽ đưa anh đến chỗ cô ấy," she instructed me. (Wait here, I will take you to her.) She went back inside the house and soon came back out with her umbrella.

"Hãy đi với tôi, ngôi nhà không xa đâu," she said. (Come with me, I'll take you there.) I followed her down the street. We walked about half a mile, twisting through streets and marketplaces until she stopped in front of a home.

"Vợ anh đang ở trong ngôi nhà đó," she said, pointing at the house. (Your wife is inside that home.) She turned and hastily walked away. I walked up to the gate and pushed it; it opened. There was no one around that I could see. I heard a pan of water splash and hit the ground from a walled area to the side of the home. I walked around the walled area to the backside of the house. I saw Thui squatting over a large plastic tub, rubbing laundry on a hand-washing board.

"Thui," I called her name. She jumped up, slung the clothes down on the ground, and ran into my arms, crying loudly.

"You came; how did you find me?" she asked. "Buddha guided me," I answered in a half-truth. "Why did you leave without telling anyone?" I asked.

"I was afraid to tell my father that your ancestors are from India," she replied.

"What do you mean? My ancestors are from England, Ireland, and France," I told her.

"But, you say your grandmother is half Indian after I tell you've got an Asian aura," she accused.

"Not India, she is Cherokee, Native American, American Indian, not from India," I informed her.

"Oh, I am so happy. I want to go home now," she said, clinging to me tightly while wiping the tears away with the sleeve of her Ao Dai. The rickshaw operator had followed me and Thui's friend to the home and was waiting for me. We climbed aboard and sat together in the seat. We rode to the bus stop with arms wrapped around each other until we drew close to the bus stop area. When we could be seen from the bus stop area, Thui pulled away from me and moved to one side of the seat.

"Good Vietnamese girls do not hold boyfriends in public. Everyone would think that I am con đi nhiều"(a slut), she explained.

"Thui, we need to get back as quickly as possible. Your parents are worried sick. Can we hire a taxi or some other type of transportation?"I asked her.

"I will ask; you wait here until I make a deal with someone. They will charge five times as much if they know you are an American," she informed me.

"If they ask, tell them that I am of French descent. I speak enough Vietnamese to get by," I instructed her. This was a tactic that saved me from capture by the Viet Cong in the coming year.

We hired a three-wheeled cart used for hauling products to the market for the equivalent of ten dollars. One hour later, we arrived at Thui's parents' home. They were so relieved to have her back home that they didn't ask any questions. Thui told them that Buddha told me where to find her. Right away, her mother started lighting incense sticks at the family's ancestral altar and giving thanks to Buddha. She went to the market and bought a black chicken to fix me a Chinese chicken dinner.

She knew that I loved her Chinese chicken dish. Her preparing the dish was her way of thanking me for finding her daughter and bringing her back home. After we had finished dinner, Mr. Vo, Thui's father, asked if I knew anyone who would sell a five-ton truck. I asked what it would be used for. He informed me that the bed and cab would be removed, and a bus would be built on the chassis. His business kept him abreast of all things related to transportation.

I told him that I did not know, but I would be on the lookout. I also asked how much money he would make from selling the truck. I was not even going to bother if hardly any money was to be made. He told me that he could make the equivalent of ten thousand dollars for a five-ton truck. I asked if there were other items that would bring good money.

He told me that he could get fifteen to twenty thousand dollars for any type of earth-moving equipment. I asked how the vehicles could be hidden from Military CID. I knew that CID would be looking under every rock and crevasse until they found any item stolen from the government. He also told me that he could make five hundred dollars for each ¼ inch by 8 feet by 4 feet steel sheet I could find. I told him the steel would not be too hard to come by.

I had a Supply Sergeant friend in charge of the S-4 yard on Dong Tam. He had once asked if I knew any Vietnamese who would buy items he had in the yard. He had mentioned that most of the construction materials in the S-4 yard were not in the books. He had told me that numerous materials were acquired or brought over by the 93rd Engineers. They brought the materials when they began construction on the compound starting in 1966.

I spent the rest of Saturday with Thui. We lay on a hammock in a room adjoining the kitchen, making out. Her younger sister became our lookout, sitting by the door and making funny kissing noises. She always enjoyed teasing me when I visited the family. Thui never let me touch her below the waist when we lay together and made out. She and her family had high moral standards due to their Buddhist and Confucian teachings.

That was one of the reasons I fell in love with her. I also came from a very religious family. My father is a Pentecostal preacher. I have two uncles who are also ministers—one is a pastor, and another is an evangelist. It would not do for me to bring home a wife with loose morals. My morals were not as they once were, but I was still a straight-laced individual. I didn't drink, smoke, or use God's name in vain. I had grown up as a strong Christian. Thui once told me that my strong faith was one of the characteristics that drew her to me.

After a couple of hours lying together, we said good night and went to bed. She slept on a mat with her three sisters atop a knee-high platform. I slept on a mat with her three brothers in a sleeping area on the opposite side of the room. The two sleeping areas were constructed the same—each was about knee height off the floor and covered by mosquito netting that zipped in the middle.

Sunday morning, we had breakfast of rice and chicken soup flavored with **Nước Mắm**, a fish sauce made from fermented anchovies. I stayed at Thui's home until around 1400 hours. Then, I walked across the street to the front gate of Camp Viking and shortly caught a ride back to Dong Tam.

****

Chapter 8

I was delighted with the news I received after I reached my barracks. My platoon sergeant informed me that we were moving to Camp Viking. He also informed me that I had been reassigned to Company B. As I mentioned earlier, the 93rd was tasked to construct most of the roads across the My Cong Delta. If all the roads they built were placed end to end, the two-lane road would reach from Washington, DC, to Las Vegas, NV. Company B's portion was to pave the roads with cold asphalt. The current project was to complete the portion of the road that Company C had begun.

I was assigned as squad leader of nine dump trucks and a maintenance vehicle. My job was to ride shotgun in the maintenance truck, also known as a Contact Truck, at the rear of the convoy. It was the wrong place to be; I must have eaten a ton of dust kicked up by the trucks at the front of the convoy. The trucks hauled asphalt from dawn to dusk.

The round trip from the asphalt plant to the job site was close to seventy miles. We usually made three to four trips each day, seven days a week. I rode in the Contact Truck, an M880 1 1/4-ton dual-wheel vehicle with toolboxes attached to each side. The vehicle carried enough tools to complete a major overhaul on any type of vehicle. It had an electric generator, an air compressor, and a welder in the rear of the vehicle. My job was to supervise the convoy and radio for help if any problems occurred during the trips.

I was very familiar with the tools. I grew up on a farm and often helped my father and uncle with repairs on farm equipment. I took an

FFA class in high school and rebuilt my first 283-cubic-inch Chevy engine at the age of 12. The mechanic was very impressed with my knowledge, especially the fact that I could easily thread a nut on a bolt without cross-threading it. After riding with the Contact Truck for six months, I was awarded a 62B20 MOS (Heavy Equipment Mechanic) after six months of on-the-job training. This was an MOS that I carried for the rest of my military career and twelve years of civilian life.

The best advantage to Thui and me was that Camp Viking was located across the street from her father's warehouse. The warehouse was approximately two hundred feet long and forty feet wide. It was constructed with galvanized tin sheets covering the top and sides. The rear of the building faced Camp Viking. It had a double door that I had never seen open during the two years I had known Thui. I didn't know what was inside. I had asked Thui once, and she told me that construction materials were inside, which were issued to the military and Civil Engineers. About fifty feet from the front of the building were the living quarters for Thui and her family. The space was divided into three sections.

In front of the building was an empty room with a couple of cabinets and a refrigerator. It was also mine and Thui's make-out room. There was a hammock hanging out of sight behind the wall. We spent many afternoons entangled in each other's arms, kissing passionately, while her younger sister stood lookout.

The center room was the largest. It served as a kitchen and living area. The seating area consisted of two large 10-foot by 6-foot knee-high platforms along each side of the wall. The platforms were covered with mosquito netting that stayed unzipped from the middle and rolled to the sides. The sleeping mats were plastic-woven mats that covered the top of the platform.

The mats also stayed rolled up during the day. One would sit on the side of the platform with their feet on the floor or in one of the cane chairs at the small kitchen table. Most meals were consumed sitting atop the platform.

The room next to the warehouse was small, with only one-bed platform. It contained Thui's parents, who slept with her eight-month-old brother. Across from the bed was a sandbagged bunker. The bunker was large enough to hold Thui, her parents, and eight of her siblings. It was tight when I had to squeeze in, as I did on numerous occasions. Charley (Viet Cong) often picked one o'clock in the morning to start lobbing mortar rounds into the ARVN Compound located behind the building.

One night, during an attack on the compound in January 1971, we stayed in the bunker through the night. The next morning, I walked into the sleeping area and noticed numerous AK-47 round holes running across and dotting the area where we usually slept. I counted seventy-eight bullet holes, all hitting within range of where we would usually sleep. This was another time I gave thanks to my praying mother back home. She surely had a connection with God, and God listened when she beseeched Him to protect me. There is a lot of power in a mother's prayers, very similar to a flak jacket.

Being stationed at Camp Viking also provided other advantages to me. I often had to go to the S-4 yard at Dong Tam to pick up building supplies for Camp Viking. One afternoon in February 1971, I made one such run. I was to contact the S-4 and have him issue the materials the compound needed to build a club for the troops.

On this day, my friend was on Supply Issue Duty. After we had loaded twelve sheets of plywood onto the rear of the vehicle, he had me drive around to a stack of 4-foot by 8-foot steel sheet metal. I noticed there were six to eight sheets in the stack.

He loaded the sheets with a forklift onto the rear of the deuce-and-a-half. He then guided me to a small shed near the edge of the Supply

Yard. Inside were two MIG wire welders with rolls of wire lying to the side. He also loaded the two pieces of equipment onto the vehicle.

"Get that stuff out of here," he instructed me.

"Why? I didn't come for all that. I was supposed to pick up sheets of 2/8 plywood to use to build a club. That's all I was to get," I replied.

"Just hurry and take the stuff and leave," he instructed once again. "Just where am I to take it?"I questioned.

"Anywhere but here. I've had that stashed away, waiting for you to come by for over a month. The items are not accounted for. Take the stuff and sell it," he again instructed.

"How much do you want to get for all that?"I asked.

"As much as you can get. You can have everything over five hundred dollars that you sell the stuff for," he informed me.

"I just got paid. I have four hundred on me now. How about I give the four hundred to you, and we'll call it even?"I offered.

"Sounds good to me. Easy money, give it here," he said, holding out his hand.

I left the S-4 yard feeling very uneasy. I knew I had to get rid of the load before I reached Camp Viking. I racked my brain, thinking of what to do with the load of material. I knew that I would not be able to unload the truck by myself. There was a small restaurant between Dong Tam and Camp Viking that Thui's father had taken me to eat at a few times. I stopped and pulled the truck off the road, pulling into a small alleyway running beside the restaurant. I noticed that there was a small covered lean-to attached to the rear of the restaurant. I pulled the truck next to the lean-to, got out, and went through the back door.

The restaurant owner recognized me at once. He asked me what I had on the truck. I told him that I had some stuff that I was talking to

Mr. Vo. I asked him if I could unload the materials and leave the load at his restaurant. He told me that it would be fine. He informed me that he and Mr. Vo always stored things for each other. He got some men to help unload the welders and steel sheets. I don't know how much money was made from the sale. Later, Thui told me that we had enough money to pay for the wedding and fix up a home that Mr. Vo had in another section of town.

Two months later, the family moved into the home. It was a much better place to live, with plenty of space and running water. Before the family moved, we dipped water out of a canal that ran beside the storage building. The water was purified by mixing chunks of chlorine into the water. I drank from the water barrel for two years without experiencing any ill effects. The water tasted much better than the water we had at Camp Viking, although it was taken from the same canal.

Thui was often stopped by the Vietnamese police, whom American servicemen referred to as White Mice. Mr. Vo insisted that Thui and I go to the Tiền Giang province magistrate office in My Tho and obtain a Vietnamese marriage license. We both thought it was a good idea. The office was located in the center of the city, a couple of blocks from the My Tho River. The magistrate knew Mr. Vo, so he went to the office with us. He was also a witness and had to sign a release stating he gave his permission for us to marry. I thought this was odd because an American woman did not need her parent's permission to marry.

Thui was already twenty years of age and old enough to decide things on her own. I was also thankful that I had taken it slow in gaining his trust. He would have never permitted during the first eight months Thui and I were dating. The license also had to be notarized by the American Embassy. Again, I was ever grateful to my company commander for providing us with the letter. I could have been court-martialed if I had not secured the permission letter before obtaining the marriage license.

After we returned home, she talked everything over with her parents, and they decided that we should go to the American Embassy the following week. Early in March of 1971, I requested and received a three-day pass to go to the American Embassy in Saigon. Thui and I made the trip on a bus traveling the same route through Tan An and Cho Lon. I asked her if she wanted to get off and visit with her employer when we stopped at the Cho Lon bus stop.

"I never want to talk about that again," she protested, giving me a hard punch on the shoulder with her fist.

"Thui, you should not treat your husband like that," berated an elderly lady sitting behind us with two chickens in a bamboo cage in her lap.

"Chào bà, bà đang đi đâu vậy (Hello, Madam, where are you traveling)?"Thui spoke, turning around in her seat to face the lady.

"Tôi đang trên đường đến Sài Gòn để thăm con trai tôi. Mẹ bạn có khỏe không? (I am going to Saigon to visit my son. Is your mother well?)" she questioned.

"Who is that lady?"I asked Thui.

"She is one of my mother's friends. She lives in the same housing complex as we do."

After she identified the woman, I remembered seeing her sitting in front of one of the homes a couple of houses near Thui and her family's home in the city. "I wondered how she knew your name," I told her. Soon, we arrived at the bus station in Saigon. The White Mice had a checkpoint set up, checking the ID cards of everyone who exited the bus. I showed them my military ID card and our marriage license. After seeing the marriage license, they waved us on.

We caught a taxi. This was the first real taxi I had ever ridden during my time in Vietnam. Thui told the driver that we wanted to go to the American Embassy. He informed us that he would drop us off a couple of blocks from the embassy but would not drive to the gate. He told us about the streets around the embassy being crowded with students protesting. I told him to take us as close as he could. After a fifteen-minute drive, he stopped and told us that this was as close as he would take us. After we exited the taxi, we walked in the direction of the embassy. We heard a loud voice shouting over a PA system. We rounded the corner, and the street ahead was full of people. I had never seen so many angry, shouting, fist-waving Vietnamese. I grabbed Thui's hand and turned around, starting to walk back down the street to where the taxi had dropped us off. There were no taxis in sight.

"We have to get out of here right now; this is not a safe place to be," I told Thui.

"The taxi is gone; how will we get away?" she asked, concern in her voice.

"I see a rickshaw sitting over there," I answered, pointing toward a vacant pedal vehicle with no driver.

We walked over to the rickshaw, but the operator was not around. I told her to sit down in the seat while I looked around for the operator. I walked a short distance down the street and stopped when I heard Thui's voice.

"Hurry! Get on! The driver came back; he will take us back to the taxi stand," she instructed.

"Thank God! We were in a lot of danger; there's no telling what those fellows would have done to us if they had noticed and chased after us," I told her, much relieved.

At the time, it was the most frightening moment of my life. I was not so worried about what would happen to me, but I was very.

concerned about the danger to Thui. I had a .45 Army pistol in a holster that I wore everywhere I went. When I first saw the crowd, I had taken the weapon from the holster. I had jacked a round into the chamber and placed it back in the holster. The rickshaw operator pedaled us to the nearest taxi stand. We hired a taxi to take us to Thui's aunt's home, who lived in Tan An. We spent a couple of days watching the news on TV.

Two days later, after all the protesters had left, we made the return trip back to the embassy. The Vietnamese lady who took all the applications for visas was very accommodating, providing all the forms and information to obtain a passport and visa for Thui to go to America. She also notarized our marriage license. When we left Saigon to return back to My Tho, Thui was so excited.

"These pieces of paper are the most valuable things I have. I need to buy a box that locks to keep them safe," she informed me.

"We will, as soon as we reach My Tho," was my reply.

"No, we are stopping at Tan An. I want to show the papers to my cousin and my aunt. My cousin doesn't believe that I am a Cherry Girl. She is a whore, and she thinks I am too. She tells me that you will never take me to America. She says all GIs tell girls they love them, then go back to America and never come back," she explained.

"You know I would never do you that way, don't you?" I asked her.

"Yes, I trust you completely. I know you would never do the same," she assured me.

These words would haunt me later on when I did have to make a return trip back to America and leave her for the longest forty-five days of my life.

****

Chapter 9

O n our way back to Tan An, we crossed a newly repaired bridge at Ben Luc. The RMK-BRJ construction company just completed the repairs on the bridge. The Ben Luc Bridge crosses the Van Co Dong River about 16 miles south of Saigon. It is the dock for the US Brown Water Navy. The base is at the junction of two rivers, and the bridge spans both rivers. I noticed much debris and steel piling lying in the river and on the north bank. Thui told me the PAVN (People's Army of Vietnam) had blown the bridge in February to disrupt the flow of supplies and ammunition to the My Cong Delta. Later, the next month, I would be assigned TDY (Temporary Duty) to the 46th Engineer Company stationed at Ben Luc to clean the area and haul away the debris. The Ben Luc naval base served the best chow of any mess hall in Vietnam. We always stopped at the mess hall when passing through the area. We arrived at Tan An, the home of Thui's aunt, around noon. Thui's cousin met us at the door.

This was the first time that we had met. She was three years Thui's elder, approximately Thui's height, but a few pounds heavier. Her hair was cut and cropped to the skin. When I noticed the haircut, my impression was that she was a Buddhist nun.

"You came back. I thought I would not see you again. My mother told me that you had married and were going to America," she stated as she opened the door and stepped aside to let us in.

"I am; we are leaving next February if we can get a visa and passport by then," Thui answered.

"Hi, I am Gia. I am Thui's only cousin," she said, holding out her hand for me to shake.

"Xin chào cô Gia, Rất vui được gặp cô,"(Hello, Miss Gia, nice to meet you) I answered, grasping her hand.

"Bạn nói tiếng việt giỏi lắm, mẹ tôi bảo tôi là bạn biết tiếng việt,"(You speak Vietnamese very well; my mother told me you speak Vietnamese) she replied, grasping my hand tighter and not letting go.

"Bạn có thể buông tay chồng tôi ra,"(You can let go of my husband's hand) Thui told her angrily.

"All cousins are alike all over the world. They are easily too jealous," I said, prying her hand loose from mine with my left hand.

"I am not jealous. Gia tries to take my things, my Ao Dia, my shoes, now she wants to take my husband," Thui complained.

"I am so happy to see you. You have a nice husband. The way he looks at you, no one can take him," she reassured her.

Her reply made me feel much easier. For a moment, I thought I might have to break up a fight between the cousins. Thui showed the marriage license, visa, and passport application to her aunt. When her cousin attempted to look at the applications, Thui hurriedly gathered the papers and placed them back inside her handbag. She informed her aunt that we must be back in My Tho before sunset. Her aunt gave Thui and me a loving hug and told us to hurry back to visit her. I was glad her cousin did not bother to hug us or shake my hand.

Thui and I walked the short distance to the Tan An bus stop. We boarded another bus on the return trip from Saigon to My Tho. We arrived in My Tho close to 1800 hours that evening. Thui's mother was pleased when Thui showed her the visa and passport applications. Her mother secured all the application papers in a lockbox in which she kept the family finances. She tucked the box tightly under her arm and told us she was going to see a lawyer. She returned after dark and informed us she had hired a lawyer to do all the paperwork. She said the fee was three hundred in MPC, equivalent to 12,425,000 Won.

My three-day pass expired Thursday, and I had to be back at my barracks by 1800 hours. I awoke early and prepared to return to the barracks. Thui and her parents had moved to the new residence. Thui's younger brother, Thanh, age 17, had remained at the Camp Viking residence to care for the property and a cow. While Thui and I were away in Saigon, Thui's mother purchased the animal to fatten and be slaughtered for the wedding. He had trouble with the Viet Cong in the area. He always took the animal out to pasture to a patch of grass at the edge of the jungle. The area was located on the east side of the Camp Viking airstrip.

Thanh was approached by a squad of Viet Cong living deep in the jungle two days before our return to My Tho. They took his picture with a Polaroid camera and warned him not to talk about them being in the area. They warned him that if he did, his home and cow would be mortared. Thanh was afraid to take the cow back to the pasture. I gave him enough money to buy a fifty-kilo bag of rice, bottles of nước mắm, and a few tins of Spam. I told him to take the supplies to the spot where the Viet Cong approached him, leave the supplies, and go back home. I advised him not to go back into the jungle again, and his parents agreed. I hoped that by making this gesture, the Viet Cong would leave him alone. He took the supplies to the spot in the jungle every month for the remainder of my tour in Vietnam.

The walk back to my barracks was a twenty-minute walk. After Thanh's encounter with the Viet Cong, I was uneasy walking down the gravel road that led from the main street to Camp Viking. There had been a few times Camp Viking received sniper fire from the area I walked through. I was always on high alert when I walked through the area. I always kept my hand resting on the grip of the .45. I had removed the round from the chamber of the weapon after the incident at the embassy. I always carried a round in the chamber and kept the holster unsnapped while walking through My Tho. This was suggested by a MACV team advisor I met back in 1970.

I walked toward the front door, slipping the weapon from my holster to inject a round in the chamber. To complete this action requires pulling the slide to the rear until it stops, then pushing the slide back in place. The round is then injected into the chamber. The next step is the most dangerous. The trigger hammer was to be lowered softly against the firing pin. The right thumb holds the trigger hammer back while the trigger is pulled. The trigger hammer is then lowered slowly to rest against the firing pin. When this last step is completed, pulling the trigger is all that is required to fire the weapon. To accomplish this action, the barrel is grasped at the end with the left hand to hold the weapon steady. I must have repeated the action at least one hundred times in the past.

On this evening, I was distracted by one of Thui's sisters. Suddenly, the hammer slipped from under my thumb and snapped forward. The hammer hit the round in the firing pin, and the round went off. The bullet bit the side of my right little finger, tearing off the flesh. I dropped the weapon on the floor and grabbed my small pinky. It was bleeding profusely; I panicked and imagined that my pinkie must be hanging on only a strip of flesh. I wrapped a bandage around my finger and asked Mr. Vo to take me to the Dong Tam Field Hospital. I climbed on the bike behind Mr. Vo on his Honda 90 motorcycle. He drove to the field hospital.

After we arrived, the doctor unwrapped the bandage to have a look at my finger. He shook his head and asked me how the incident happened. I told him it was an accident and how it happened. He told me that it was only a flesh wound and that I must have a mental deficit to carry around a cocked-loaded .45. I did not mention to him about the two grenades that I often carried on each side of the web belt. I would secure the grenades with the safety levers with the safety pins removed, then wrap rubber bands around the top to hold the safety levers in place.

The Army doctor mentioned to me that more accidents happened with loaded weapons than unloaded weapons. When he mentioned this fact, I thought of hoping that the MACV team member who taught me the trick blew his finger off. The worst that came from the accident was that the round had passed through the wall of a neighbor's home and burst a hanging crucifix. The doctor bandaged my finger and told me to keep it clean for a few days. I still have a scar on my left pinky. It is the only round that hit me during my three years of tours in Vietnam.

I had instructed Mr. Vo to return after he dropped me off at the hospital. He had a Civil Service ID card that gave him entrance to the compound. The same card would cause his arrest and his death by the NVA after the fall of Saigon in 1975. He had hidden the card along with the M1911A1 Colt .45 in the cubby of the bunker in his home. The NVA searched all the houses after they finally reached My Tho. Mr Vo's home was searched, and two contraband items were discovered; he was arrested and placed in an NVA reeducation camp. After two years of beatings and hard labor, he died.

I had a bunk in the NCO hooch in the 93rd Headquarters area. After dinner, I went to the 65th Transportation Company to play cards with the truck drivers. I stopped playing cards with troops in my own company after the incident with a sergeant the year prior. It was more fun winning a few dollars from other troops than winning money from my friends. I also made a habit of stopping if I lost more than twenty dollars.

On this evening, I sat in on a card game with three individuals. After we played for a while, I noticed one of the individuals was losing a lot. Another driver asked me if I was the sergeant from the 93rd who spoke Vietnamese. I told him that I could speak a little Vietnamese. He said he thought so, that his hooch maid had once pointed me out to him. I played cards for a couple of hours, then told them I was quitting and went back to my barracks. The driver, who had been losing heavily at cards, got up and followed me back to my barracks. He stopped me at the door and said he wanted to discuss something with me. I looked inside the hooch and noted that no one was in the room. I invited him in. He sat in a metal folding chair beside my bunk while I sat on the edge of my bunk.

"My hooch maid told me that you knew a Vietnamese Masan in town who will buy black market items," he questioned.

"I don't know anyone, but my wife's father might know someone," I answered back.

"What items can I sell to make enough money to bother coping it?" he inquired.

"Ah, well, let's see. My father-in-law once mentioned that a five-ton vehicle would get as much as ten thousand dollars," I replied.

"Well, that is something to think about. I do know where there is a five-ton dump truck sitting, ready to be sold," he informed me.

I was a bit taken aback by his boldness and a little concerned that he might be setting me up to be busted by the CID (U.S. Army Criminal Investigation Command). I didn't know whether to tell him anything else. Therefore, I told him to come see me next Monday, and we would discuss the matter. What I really wanted to do was talk to Mr. Vo and ask how he could make it happen without the two of us getting caught.

I returned to Thui's home Saturday morning. As usual, Thui's younger brothers and sisters met me halfway down the lane. They helped me carry cases of Fanta orange pop down the lane to the home. Although Vietnam had orange soda that tasted better than the PX sodas, the kids loved PX orange soda. Mr. Vo was home when we all got to the house. I set the cases of soda aside and sat at the table across from him. I told him about my conversation with the truck driver the day before. He thought for a while and told me to have the person drive the truck and park it beside a small café about half a mile outside the front gate. The driver was to go inside the café and wait while leaving the engine running. After sitting for twenty minutes, an ARVN sergeant would approach him and hand him an envelope. He was to check the contents of the envelope to see if five hundred in MPC notes were inside. If the amount was correct, he was to walk back to the front gate and report to the guard on duty that someone had driven off with his truck while he was sitting in the café eating lunch. I did not ask Mr. Vo what would happen to the truck. I did not want to know anything else about the deal after I relayed the message to the driver. I never heard anything from the truck driver after I gave him the message. I guess everything went according to plan.

When I returned to my barracks on Monday, the First Sergeant informed me that I was to go with the First Platoon to Ben Luc. My job was to be an interpreter for Vietnamese nationals hired to help move all the steel and debris around the bridge. Ben Luc Bridge spans the junction of the Vam Co Tay and Vam Co Dong rivers along Highway 4.

The town of Ben Luc is mostly populated with rice farmers and nationals who worked at Army Camp Ben Luc or the naval base beside the river. Seabees constructed the base to provide support facilities for the Brown Water Navy Patrol boats. The Seabees had constructed a base defense system of towers and barbed wire fence around the perimeter. They also constructed ammunition storage bunkers, a helicopter pad, maintenance facilities, troop barracks, and a mess hall. After the naval base construction was completed, 812 men worked at the base. At the time, there were seventy vessels tied up at the dock or anchored in the middle of the river's junction.

Most of the Seabees and navy personnel had departed the base by the time the First Platoon was tasked with the cleanup. We took over the barracks vacated by the Navy personnel. Our first task was to complete major repairs on the barracks and perimeter defenses. After the naval personnel vacated the base, the Vietnamese came in and removed everything they could carry. We hired Vietnamese nationals to do the repairs. It was my job to use my language skills to supervise and give them directions. Many of the women had worked on the base when the Navy occupied it. Since I could speak Vietnamese and understand the culture, all fell in love with me right away. I told them that I was married to a Vietnamese who lived in My Tho.

They told me that Vietnamese men could have three or four wives and that my wife would understand if I had a wife in their town. I would laugh and tell them that not if they had a wife like mine; they would become widows once she discovered them. They all had heartbreaking stories about GIs declaring their love for them. After they fell in love with a GI, he soon left and never returned. My resolve drastically increased after hearing their stories of heartache; I was more determined to do all that was needed to take Thui back to the States with me.

Thui came to visit me at least once a week during the two months I was away on the cleanup detail. All of the women hated her because she never stayed the night. They would tell me if Thui really loved me, she would stay clean and cook for me. They all knew that I had a room to myself in the barracks. There had been a few times when one of them would slip in at night and crawl into my bed. That stopped after I threw all of them out of my room and fired the women the next day.

It took two months for the first platoon to complete the Ben Duc Bridge cleanup detail. While we were away, B Company moved from Camp Viking to a vacated Seabee compound two miles west of My Tho alongside the My Cong River. The location was ideal for Thui and me. It was a ten-minute walk to the family's new residence. In addition, the walk was towards My Tho, and the route was in a more secure area of the city. After I returned, my duty assignment was Permanent Sergeant of the Guard. I would have this duty assignment for the remainder of my tour in Vietnam.

Company B hired national locals to serve as hooch maids, kitchen staff, and other tasks that GIs often completed. Each troop chipped in twenty dollars each month. The price was low since we were no longer required to do kitchen duties, clean our rooms, or burn waste in barrels. My Sergeant of the Guard duties included checking workers' ID cards and bags when they entered the compound in the mornings. I checked their bags again when they left in the evening.

They walked through a short hall that ran along beside the gate. I had a box set at the entrance for the workers to drop in contraband before they left the compound. If I saw anyone place anything in the box, I would question them about how they acquired the item. If I determined that the item was present, I would return it to them. Many workers received cartons of cigarettes and other items troops would purchase for them from the PX.

Many top NCOs often gave their hooch maids gifts. This system worked well for me through the rest of my tour. Items were rarely stolen from us. The Vietnamese, in general, were trustworthy. GIs stole from each other much more than the locals stole from the troops. I also had to pull perimeter defense duties every three nights. I would work three days on and three days off. This was more time off than that of other sergeants. The three-day rotation also allowed me to go home more often and presented easier opportunities to complete paperwork.

The Seabee compound was set up to be easy to defend. The north side was situated next to an ARVN compound. A tall barbed fence was constructed around the compound to separate the two. The front of the compound faced the road that ran from My Tho to Ben Tre. Rice paddies were on the east side of the compound. This area was the hardest to defend. A twenty-foot-tall guard tower was constructed on both ends of the compound. Guards manned machine gun positions in both towers during the night. The towers were empty and not guarded during the day. This practice changed a few months later when the Viet Cong attacked a Vietnamese Reserve unit compound located about five miles west of the compound. The attack left all 25 troops stationed at the compound dead. After this event, tower guards remained on high alert for the next four months.

I had traded my M1922 .45 Colt to a black friend for his Thompson submachine gun. I felt safer carrying the Thompson when I walked through the streets of My Tho. He liked the Colt because it was easier to buckle on his waist and made it easier to climb to the guard tower platform. We both had the same duty rotation and switched back when we moved to a different compound. It was customary for construction engineers to set up base camps close to job sites.

This limited travel to and from sites. It also was safer and more feasible, limiting vehicles and heavy equipment travel through congested areas. Many roads were only oxen trails along rice paddies before they were graveled and widened. The roads were too narrow for vehicles to pass; therefore, turnarounds needed to be built at the edge of rice paddies. Many times, I had to drive backward for miles due to approaching vehicles failing to yield to my oncoming vehicle.

The week before Thui and I had planned to have our wedding ceremony, I was sent to supervise the Ben Lock Bridge project. Now that things had returned to normal and I had returned home, we decided to go ahead with the ceremony. The ceremony would be held in the ARVN compound mentioned previously. It took a week to prepare the food and make all the wedding ceremony arrangements. I had to go to a tailor and have a suit made. Thui's parents also had to complete many last-minute preparations. All the visa and passport applications were completed and returned to the embassy clerk. I was off duty from Monday to Thursday of that week. Therefore, I had a chance to take the forms to the American embassy. I asked to borrow a jeep from the motor pool to take the trip. My First Sergeant told me that I had to have a troop-riding shotgun. One of the supply clerks asked to take the ride with me. While on the road, he asked if we could stop at a place between Cho Lon and Saigon. He told me he knew one of the mama-sans who owned a small roadside restaurant in the area. We stopped and parked the jeep off the road when we arrived and went inside. I didn't speak Vietnamese to anyone when we went to a table and sat down. After I ordered a bread and meat long bun sandwich and a Coke, the supply clerk did not order anything. He walked to the back of the restaurant and talked with the mama-san.

"Đưa anh ta đến ổ thuốc phiện," she instructed one of the girls sitting on a stool beside the back entrance. (Take him back out to smoke heroin.) The young lady came over to him and took his hand.

"I'm going out back for a Boom-boom," he let me know that he was going to have sex.

"Hurry and finish your business; we have to go shortly," I instructed him. I completed my meal and waited for approximately thirty minutes for him to return. When he did not, I decided to go out back and look for him.

"Mama-San, where did the GI go?"I asked in English.

"He in room asleep," she told me, pointing to a row of shanty huts along a boardwalk leading to the Saigon River. I walked up to the doors of the first two huts and pounded on the flimsy tin door. I did not get an answer, so I continued down the board to the third hut. I didn't bother to announce myself this time; I opened the unlocked door and stepped inside. He was lying on a cot smoking a pipe. He looked at me through glazed eyes.

"Ah, Sarge, you got to try some of this; it's a killer," he said, holding out the pipe and offering it to me.

"That's shit that I don't use; get yourself together and let's get away from here," I instructed.

"Ah, man! You're killing my buzz. I will wait here; pick me up when you come back."

"Suit yourself," I told him, not saying that I would stop on the way back. I left him lying propped up on one elbow, holding the pipe to his mouth with the other hand. I walked back down the boardwalk through the restaurant and back to the jeep. I started the jeep and continued my way to Saigon. I had traveled about five miles when I noticed an MP Patrol Duck coming towards me. I pulled over to the roadside and flagged the vehicle down as it drew close to me. The vehicle stopped on the road beside me.

"Hey sarge, you having trouble?" the passenger asked. He was wearing an MP armband. The rank on his collar indicated that he was a Staff Sergeant.

"It's not me; I stopped with a guy a few miles back at one of those roadside sandwich shops. While I was eating, he went with a hooker to some huts behind the restaurant. I waited for thirty minutes, and he did not come back. I then went to check on him and found him in the third hut behind the restaurant, smoking dope. He was stoned, high as a kite. I think he's smoking heroin," I informed the MP.

"I know where the place is that you stopped. We'll stop and check on him," said the MP as they drove on in the direction I had just come from. I continued to the embassy and gave the applications to the embassy clerk. She told me to come back with Thui in three weeks to pick up her passport and visa. It was late in the afternoon after I left the embassy. I decided to stay the night in Saigon. I left my jeep at the American Embassy and caught a taxi to the Majestic Hotel. The hotel was built in 1925 by a wealthy Cho Lon Chinese businessman. The French used the hotel as a headquarters building during the 1948 French-Indochina War. During the French occupation of Vietnam, two more stories were added. The hotel had four stories, and my room was on the fourth floor. This was the floor that most GIs stayed on due to a bar located on the east side of the wing. I had a steak dinner in the bar lounge. After dinner, I sat and drank a couple of beers. This was the first beer I had drunk since I met Thui. She did not approve. I think it was because she watched her father's complete change from a loving father to a mean drunk when he drank. I noticed a slot machine sitting against the wall. I was bored and had a few 50-dong coins in my pocket. I walked over to the slot machine and fed it a 50-dong coin. Suddenly, a red light started flashing on the wall above the machine, and a siren started wailing. I was shocked as coins started spilling from a slot trough protruding from the front of the machine. I pulled my Boone hat from my head and placed it under the slot trough. My hat quickly filled up. I started gathering the coins with my hands and stuffing them in all the pockets.

A young boy about fourteen years of age came out from behind the bar with a trash can. He placed the trash can under the slot trough. The trash can was three-quarters full before the coins stopped falling. I poured the coins from my hat into the trash, then emptied most of the coins I had in my pockets into the trash can. The coins were so heavy that my fatigue pants were falling. I never knew the value of the money that was in the trash can. I had the boy carry the trash can back to my room. I only kept one pocket full of coins. I never counted the coins. I told the boy that he could have the trash full of coins. He told me that the hotel manager would take them from him after I left the hotel. I emptied the coins into a pillowcase and told him to come to my room in the morning, and I would carry the coins outside to the taxi.

The next morning, I carried the coins out of the hotel to a taxi standing by for passengers. I got in the cab and waited for about fifteen minutes. The boy from the night before showed up. I gave him the bag of coins. He opened the bag and poured out a pile of coins on the cab seat. He told the driver he was paying my taxi fare to the American Embassy. This was the last time that I ever saw the boy, and I hope he had as much luck in the future as he did on the night he met me.

****

Chapter 10

I returned to My Tho from my trip to the Embassy on Thursday afternoon. I dropped the jeep off at the motor pool. I walked to the first Sergeant's office to let him know that I was back. I asked if I could put up the wedding invitation notice on the duty assignment bulletin board. He asked when I was having the wedding. I informed him that it was tomorrow that we would have a private Buddhist marriage ceremony early in the morning. The reception would start at 12 noon and last until everyone left. He said he would announce the evening company staffing meeting. He mentioned that the CO and a couple of Lieutenants would like to attend and asked if I would restrict the reception to only ranks of E-5 and above. I told him that Thui's father had a section set aside for VIPs and that we would use that area for NCOs and officers. I also mentioned I had friends from RMB-RKJ, ARVN Officers, and NCOs.

He asked about the reception area size. I told him where we were having it, and he was pleased with the arrangements Thui's father had made, especially regarding security. I explained there would be a ton of food prepared by some of the best chefs in My Tho, mentioning the three cavies, six pigs, one hundred ducks, and one hundred chickens. There would also be a pallet of Budweiser, a whiskey bar, and all the Triger and 33 beers one could drink.

He commented on how wealthy Thui's family must be or suggested I might have been profiting from the black-market. I assured him that was not the case, explaining the money came from my military pay savings and contributions from Thui's parents. The wedding cost approximately $5000 MPC dollars in Vietnamese currency. He made me somewhat uneasy by informing me I had to go to Don Tam on Monday to see the battalion commander.

After meeting with the first sergeant, I returned to Thui's house. She had arranged a haircut appointment for me with a local beautician. Thui's mother had picked up my suit from the tailor; everything was set for the next morning. Her mother showed me where Thui and I would sleep on our wedding night, setting up a bed with clean, snow-white sheets to symbolize Thui's purity. With that in mind, I went to the boy's room and went to sleep.

When I awoke, I went to the ARVN restaurant, where Thui and her family were gathered. A private room was set aside for the wedding ceremony. Thui's mother was busy preparing for the early morning ceremony, informing me that I shouldn't eat breakfast because I'd be full by the end of the day. She told me it was tradition for me to sample each of the 12 dishes prepared.

Thui's mother had set up an ancestral altar with a large Buddha statue surrounded by offerings. Two tall, decorated candles were placed on each end to be lit by both the bride and groom as a symbol of a long and fruitful marriage. Thui's family from Hue followed different traditions, including the layered Áo dài gowns in white, dark blue, and red.

Our wedding ceremony was simple. In the private room, Thui's mother rang a Buddha mindfulness bell, and her younger brother played a wooden instrument. Thui's father lit incense and read the Five Awarenesses doctrine. Thui and I exchanged vows and wedding rings, finally lighting the candles together. Despite the intended privacy, children peered in from outside, and neighbors crowded in. Afterward, we moved everyone out to the reception area.

Over one hundred guests attended. There was a DJ, and the music was lively. NCOs, officers, RMK-BRJ friends, and other Vietnamese officials filled the VIP area while AVN troops mingled in the main area. A ten-course meal was served, starting with Thịt kho tàu (braised and caramelized pork belly with eggs), followed by various pork, beef, duck, and chicken dishes with vegetables and rice. My CO commented on the quality of the dishes. The reception lasted well into the night, with many guests enjoying themselves to the point of passing out. Despite the crowd, there were no fights. Many troops later said it was the best time they'd had in Vietnam.

Thui and I went to bed around midnight, nervous but passionate. Due to the noise and lack of privacy, we decided to sneak into her sister's room but soon returned to her parent's room to honor the tradition of proving her purity. The passion between us lasted through the night, and in the morning, Thui presented the sheet to her mother.

On Monday, I returned to the company area and met with the first sergeant. He informed me I was being temporarily assigned to the 34th Engineer Battalion at Phu Loi. Though I hadn't operated a 290M often, I agreed. I stopped by Thui's house to inform her of my assignment, and she insisted on coming with me.

We traveled from My Tho, through Vinh Long, Can Tho, and Binh Thuy, to Phu Loi, where I was to meet with the battalion commander. I dropped Thui off at a restaurant before heading into the 93rd Headquarters building. The Colonel complimented me on a report of my assistance in uncovering a heroin smuggling ring, although I'd only reported a troop smoking in an opium den. I was given a letter of commendation for my efforts, and we discussed the drug issues affecting GIs in Vietnam.

I returned to pick up Thui, and we continued to Phu Loi, stopping for the night in Tan An at her aunt's home. The next day, we registered with the local magistrate in Phu Loi. He assisted in finding us a two-room furnished apartment, which would become our home. I left Thui at the apartment and reported to the 34th Engineer, bunking with the Earth Moving Platoon.

At the job site, my task involved operating a steel wheel roller compacting fill for the road – a monotonous task. After a few days, I learned how to leave the base without detection.

I awoke the next morning thinking that I might have some time during the day to stop off at the apartment. The 34th assigned project that I had been sent to was to help complete the widening and lengthening the highway QL 13 leading to Thui Hoa. The 290M Earthmovers were being used to remove topsoil from dig pits and use the fill for the road. When I arrived at the job site, they really didn't need me, and I couldn't understand why I was sent TDY. Most of the time I ran a steel wheel roller up and down the road, compacting fill added to the road. Operating a roller is the most boring job there is on a road construction site.

It was three days before I was able to slip off the base and go to our apartment. Phu Loi was the most difficult base to leave from after 1800 hours. It was close to 1900 hours before we returned to the base each day. One day, I heard one of the equipment operators ask if he was going downtown to a local bar after work. I asked how he got off the post without being discovered. He told me that he went through an ARVN compound adjacent to our base.

He asked me if I wanted to go off base with them that evening. I told him that I did and that my wife had just rented an apartment in the town. I told him that I was worried about her and was sure she was as concerned about me. I told him we had made contact since we arrived. The guy told me to follow him out that evening and that I would be able to come and go anytime I liked. The troop came to my room after the sun went down and asked if I was ready to go. I told him to lead the way, and I would follow. He led us to the west side of the base, away from the helipads. A high chain link separated the Phu Loi base from an ARVN base built beside it. Engineers had built a gate of the same material to make an egress way through the ARVN base. It was getting dark when we approached the entrance. A path was beaten down, leading through the grass up to the exit. A jeep with a couple of MPs sitting in the front seats, had the egress way blocked. We stopped across the road that ran in front of the entrance, staying hidden in the shadows of a building.

"We will wait here until the MP jeep moves on. They stay about fifteen minutes at this spot, then move on to patrol the perimeter of the base," he informed me.

We stood waiting for a few more minutes. The driver started the vehicle engine and drove away. We walked down the beaten path to the gate. My companion removed a piece of flat metal from his pocket and inserted it in the lock that held a chain together, securing the gate. He removed the lock and chain, opened the gate, and we slipped through the gate into the ARVN base.

"We removed all the tumblers from the lock the last time we worked on the fence. The lock will open with anything that is flat and will fit the hole. When you come through, just close the gate and replace the lock and chain. No one has discovered that the lock opens without a key," he informed me while resecuring the gate.

We continued through the ARVN base without being detained. We came to another gate, much like the gate we just came through. My companion handed a pack of cigarettes to the guard standing in front of the gate. After egressing the entrance, it was a short distance from Phu Loi village.

"Don't forget to bring a pack of cigarettes to give to the guards. Keep walking on down the road, and it will come out on the street with all the bars. I am going to see my girlfriend down that street," he informed me as he turned and walked off.

I continued into Phu Loi. It was easy to find the street and locate our apartment. Thui had the door to the apartment locked. I banged on it, calling out her name. She hurriedly came to the door, opened it, and threw herself into my arms. Her eyes were red from crying.

"Why did you not come back? I was so worried something happened to you. I hate this place. When can we go back to My Tho?" she asked.

"Give me two weeks, and I will think of something. They don't really need me. I will make an excuse to return back to My Tho," I reassured her.

I knew that I had to be back inside the Phu Loi base before 2400 hours. My companion had instructed me to meet him at a bar that GIs always frequented; they all left together and went back to the compound in a group. I explained this to Thui. Neither of us was too happy that we had to separate again, but we knew that we had to be careful. I stayed with her until 2345 hours, kissed her goodbye, and walked down to the bar. My companion was waiting for me.

"I was concerned when you did not show up," he said in a relieved voice.

"I did not want to come back. If I had stayed the night, I probably would have gone AWOL. My wife was worried sick," I answered.

We made it back to the base without any difficulties. I followed the same routine each night. I was working on a plan to leave Phu Loi and go back to the 93rd in the Delta. During the second week of my TDY assignment, I decided to return to the base early. Thui's cousin from Tan An was visiting, so I decided to leave them alone to visit. It was about 2200 hours when I stopped off at the bar.

I entered the bar and noticed a full-bird Colonel and a Sergeant Major sitting at one of the tables. They had 1st Cav patches on their sleeves, and the colonel was wearing a black Stetson with crossed swords on the front. I sat down at a table next to them. The Mama san that owned the bar knew me from the few times I visited. She sat down at my table, and we started a conversation in Vietnamese. After we talked for about ten minutes, the colonel came to the table and sat down with us.

"You speak fluent Vietnamese. Where did you learn to speak that well? Are you a MAC advisor?" he inquired.

"No, sir. I am an engineer on TDY to the 34th. This is my third tour in Vietnam. I have married a Vietnamese national, and we are scheduled to return to the States in February of next year. She has her passport and visa; we are just waiting for my DEROS date," I answered.

"Did you know that the NVA has a bounty of fifty thousand dollars on the head of any American that speaks fluent Vietnamese?" he asked.

"No, sir, I did not. I will try extra hard to make sure that they don't collect the bounty on mine," I answered.

"Well, sitting in a bar alone like this without a weapon is one sure way for them to collect the bounty. Where are you from back in the world?" he inquired.

"I'm from northeast Arkansas. The Arkansas State Redskins are my favorite team," I answered.

The sergeant major came to the table and sat with us. We sat and talked for a while about football, mainly about the Arkansas Razorbacks and the game with Texas. A tape of the game was sent to Vietnam after it was played. I lost twenty dollars to a Texan because most of us didn't know the score before watching the game. Anyway, I would have put my money on the Razorbacks regardless. After a while, I looked at my wristwatch to check the time. It was 2300 hours.

Suddenly, the door of the bar was roughly thrown open, and a squad of MPs came scurrying into the place. They spread out and started searching the bar, checking for passes and ID cards. They came to our table and told the colonel that they had rounded up two squads of VC in homes a few blocks away. I was concerned and asked if any of the detainees mentioned being married to a GI. He told me that none had and that most were men, NVA and Viet Cong.

He said they had gotten a heads-up from the mayor. The MP first sergeant in charge told us it was imperative to return to the base immediately. He looked at me and asked what outfit I was from. The Colonel answered for me. He told the MP that I was a MAC advisor and that I was with him. He told the MP that they would give me a ride back to the base. I did not go to the job site the next day. I was concerned about Thui's safety and planned to go into the village in the morning. Around 0900 hours, a jeep pulled up in front of the CO's office, and an MP got out, walked inside, waited a few minutes, then got back in the jeep and drove away. A few minutes later, the company clerk ran over to the barracks. He stuck his head inside.

"Sargent Gray, do you have a Vietnamese wife?" he asked. "Yes, I do. Why, is something wrong?"I inquired.

"You'd better get to the main gate; she's down there raising hell, demanding to see you. She's threatening to go to the American authorities and get help if she doesn't get to see you," he informed me.

"Thanks a lot. I'll get my hat and the jeep I came in and go to the front gate right away," I reassured him.

I drove to the front gate and noticed Thui was standing by the guard with her suitcase in her hand. I stopped the jeep, and she got in. I drove back to the orderly room and told the First Sergeant that my wife had a family emergency and that I had to return to My Tho. He informed me that I could stay, that they did not need me, and that he was going to send me back the next Monday. We drove back to the apartment and gathered the remainder of her belongings. We arrived in My Tho at 1600 hours. I did not return the jeep back to the motor pool. I parked it inside a building Mr. Vo sometimes used to store supply items. He asked me if I wanted to sell the vehicle. I told him that Thui and I had stopped our black market activities; we did not want to take any more chances of being caught.

****

Chapter 11

I returned to Ben Tri on Monday morning around 1000 hours and checked in with the B company's First sergeant. Yes, I took the jeep back to the motor pool. I did not sell it. The company had changed commanding officers while I was on TDY at Phu Loi. He came from one of the 93rd-line companies. He had recently been promoted to captain, and Company B was his first command. The first Sergeant informed me that he wanted to meet with me. I walked to the back of the orderly room to his doorless office. I knocked on the side of the door frame. He motioned for me to come on into his office. I walked in and stepped in front of his desk.

"Sir Sargent Gray reporting as directed," saluting sharply.

"Have a seat. I have something I want to discuss with you," he informed me while motioning at a metal folding chair sitting across the room against the wall.

"Sir, what can I do for you?"I inquired after sitting down.

"The first Sergeant tells me that you speak fluent Vietnamese," he stated.

"Yes, Sir, I am fair fluent. I learned to read and write Vietnamese; I studied a Monterey Language course during my first six months in the country. Since then, I have become fluent enough that I can converse with Vietnamese just about anything. I can easily understand what is being said on Vietnamese TV," I replied.

"Company B is hiring Vietnamese workers to help widen the road from Thot Not to Can Tho. Can you go along and supervise the Vietnamese crew," he inquired.

"Sir, I don't think I would have a problem with that. I have supervised working crews for the past two years," I assured him.

"Well, then you are hired. I am sending you to Thot Not. Get your gear together and catch a ride over there with the earthmoving platoon," he instructed.

"Sir, could I have a few days to put things in order before I leave? I just got married and need some time to prepare my wife for another TDY assignment," I requested.

"I heard about your wedding. Wish you had invited me," he stated.

"Sir, I would have had I known you wanted to come," I assured him.

"I did not know about the wedding until after the fact. Your last CO said the food was the best he has ever had, especially the lobsters. He said that they must have weighed two pounds each. You can leave next week. Take your wife with you if you want. She can stay on the compound until you locate dwellings for her." he informed me.

"Sir, Thanks a lot. I will do my best."I assured him as I got up and left the orderly room.

I went back to the room I shared with another NCO. I packed my duffle bag with all the remaining field gear I had processed. I lost most of it a year ago. The only field gear I had remaining was a helmet liner with a steel pot, a web belt with ammo pouches and a flak Jacket. This was the usual TA 50 inventory that most long-timers carried. Everything else was either lost or stolen. Lost field gear was written off as a combat loss. I arranged for my locker and bunk to be moved with the platoon. I decided to take a shower before going back to Thui's home. The only way I could shower at home was the

Vietnamese way, stripped down, using a water hose and squatting behind a screen partition. The shower on the base was not much better and the water was ice cold when taking a morning shower.

The company shower arrangement was a five-hundred-gallon water tanker setting on top of a ten-foot high platform with the sides closed plastic sheeting. Mirrors were attached on the sides, and four shower spickets hung from overhead. Most troops waited until afternoon to shower, to give the water time to be warmed by the sun. The water trailer held only five hundred gallons of water and was required to be refilled each day. The hooch maids washing clothes used much of the water every day. I gathered all my belongings and civilian clothes and stuffed them in a laundry bag. I wore my jungle fatigues because I was carrying my M-16. Troops carrying weapons clothed in civilian attire were too concupiscible.

When I arrived at the Vo's home, her mother informed me that Thui had gone to Tan An. She had told me before I went to work that she wanted to visit her aunt and cousin. I informed Mrs. Vo about having to make the move to Thot Not. She suggested that I take Thui with me and locate a place for us to live. She also wanted me to go to the Post Exchange on Dong Tam and look for a pioneer stereo system.

She told me that she had a friend willing to pay $1500.00 in MPC for a complete sound system. I told her that I didn't have transportation to bring the system home after I purchased it. She suggested that I use Mr. Vo's Honda 90 Motorcycle for transportation. I thought for a while and went outside to look at the motorbike. I have ridden the motorcycle on numerous occasions in the past. Mr Vo had prefabbed a holder that was attached to the rear of the set. Mrs Vo had opened a small house appliances shop in the My Tho marketplace. He used the attachment to haul goods from Saigon to My Tho. I thought I could use the motorbike to transport the sound system if I made two trips. Mrs. Vo gave me some MPC notes with which to make the purchase, and I rode the motorbike to Dong Tam exchange. The first trip was easy.

I strapped the receiver and a tape player to the motorcycle and transported the items back home without any problems. It was after 1700 hours when I made the last trip to bring back the speakers. I did not have any trouble strapping the speakers to the motorbike. However, they did protrude six inches above my head. The motorbike was unbalanced and shuddered, making it hard to control.

On my last trip, the sun had set, and it was getting dark. I was uneasy traveling the road after dark. The route took me through the same area where the VC ambush had occurred in 1970. After I had traveled a short distance from Dong Tam, I approached an ID checkpoint manned by an ARVN Reserve unit. I slowed to a stop at the checkpoint. A troop grabbed the handlebars of the motorcycle and told me to dismount. That was one thing that I was not going to do.

I spoke to him in Vietnamese and told him that he did not have the authority to stop me. He tapped his rifle and told me that the rifle was the only authority he needed. When he said that, I knew that there was going to be trouble. I gunned the engine and gave him a karate chop across his collarbone. He screamed and let go of the handlebars.

I let go of the clutch and spinout, slinging gravel all over them. I heard rapid rifle fire as I drove away. The rounds flew over my head; they must have been poor marksman, or they were just trying to frighten me. I hightailed away from the area and returned home. Later, Mrs Vo told me that I broke the collarbone of the troop with the karate chop. She had to pay for the doctor's bill. The ARVN reserves at the roadblock must have known who I was. It did not take much time for me to be found since almost everyone in My Tho knew who I was. That was the last time I participated in black market activities.

I stayed the night at Thui's parents' home, sleeping with her brothers. The next morning, I had Mr. Vo give me a ride to the bus station and bought a ticket to Tan An. The vehicle I boarded was a country bus; it had goods and items strapped to the top. Most of the passengers were returning to their farms in the country. They were carrying items they purchased in the city across their laps or sitting on the seat beside them. I boarded the bus, holding my M16 by the carrying handle. I had my Army 45 colt in a holster strapped to my side. I went to the rear of the bus and sat in a seat behind a lady with two chickens in her lap. She was holding them by the legs. They looked like they might try to escape from her as I walked past.

I have a phobia of anything that has a beak and wings. The phobia was caused by my parental grandmother's goose and ganders. She raised the fowls to clean grass from the cotton fields. At age three, I would follow her to the cotton patches. The geese would chase me, grab me by my shirt collar and beat me with their wings. This was terrifying to a child three years old. When it happens unexpectedly, it is also terrifying to an adult age twenty-two; I had dozed off, letting M16 rest between my knees. The barrel was pointed towards the top of the bus.

My finger was resting inside the trigger guard. I had chambered a round earlier and had put the weapon's safety lever in place. Suddenly, I was awoken from my doze by one of the chickens the old lady was holding. The fowl broke loose from her and landed on top of my head. My reaction was to flip the safety off with my thumb and pull the trigger. I fired off three rounds into the top of the bus before I became wide awake. Everyone on the bus was ducking for cover. I called out in Vietnamese that the weapon firing was an accident.

I explained that I had fallen asleep and fired the weapon when I was surprised. The bus driver had stopped the bus to inquire about what had happened. He was going to kick me off the bus until I gave him fifty dollars in MPC notes. I arrived in Tan An about thirty minutes later. Thui and I spent the night at her aunt's. Her cousin's hair had grown out to medium length. Thui had once explained the reason her hair was cropped short the first time we met. Her cousin had run away from home with an ARVN soldier. The soldier had girlfriends in other villages; she found out about the other women and left him. After she returned home, her father shaved her hair to the skin with hair clippers. The family told everyone that she was at temple training to be a Buddhist nun. Her mother told all her friends that she did not like being a nun left the training, and returned home. Saving face is very important to the Vietnamese; they will go to extreme lengths to do so.

I had intended to continue with Thui to Thot Not the next day. However, Thui's aunt had other plans to take us to a floating Buddhist monastery. The monastery was a few miles from Mt. Tho, located on a small island in the middle of My Cong River. The legend is from four hundred years ago; a sect of monks was traveling down the river in a large sampan. The boat was sinking in the middle of the river. The monks beseech Budda to save them from their peril. Suddenly, the ground rose up from below and lifted the boat out of the water. The legend goes on that monks built a temple on the spot. Thui's maternal uncle resided at the monastery. He had sent a message that he wanted Thui and me to visit him.

We caught a river taxi from the dock at My Tho and hired it to take us to the monastery. After we arrived at the monastery, the monks invited our party to have lunch with them. They were impressed that I could speak Vietnamese. Some of them could speak English and wanted to converse with me in English. The food was bland, and the meal consisted of only vegetable dishes. The monks did not serve meat or fish with the meal. I had become accustomed to eating any type of Vietnamese, so I managed. After lunch, we followed him to his room. The room was about the size of a small closet with a mat folded against the wall.

He laid spread the mat on the bamboo floor and we sat down on top. He told me that he had a charm that the monks blessed for two years. He wanted to give it to me. The charm was to keep me safe from harm, he instructed me that I need to wear it always. He told me and Thui the charm would not work if I ate certain foods. He gave Thui a list of foods that were mostly green vegetables. I remember wild onions and leeks being on the list. That was fine with me since I did not care much for those vegetables anyway.

After he told me the diet limitations for the charm, I realized why Thui's family never ate leaks or wild onions. He also told me that the charm was a wedding present. He pulled the charm from the fold of his robe. It was a tiger tooth encased in 18-carat gold attached to a ten-ounce 24-carat gold chain. I kept the cham for many years. Later, we went inside the temple to pray. The prayer consisted of the ritual of kneeling before a statue of Budda one thousand times. It reminded me of a time when a girlfriend took me to visit a catholic church; only my kneecaps were much redder and sorer. We returned to Tan An later in the afternoon. Thui's aunt decided that the three of them would travel to Thot Not the next day. She thought Thui could locate an apartment or home much cheaper if I were not with them.

I returned to the compound to wait for a ride to Thot Not job site. The First Sergeant informed me that my ride had left earlier and that I would have to wait another week. I had no intention of waiting another week before arriving in Thot Not. Thui would be extremely worried if I did not show up on time as promised. The next morning, I awoke and decided that I would go to Dong Tam and catch a ride to Can Tho with a military vehicle.

I spent most of the day sitting by the main gate, stopping vehicles and asking if they were going to Can Tho. I decided to give up around 1300 hours and catch the next ride that came through the gate. I caught a ride with an ARVN vehicle going into My Tho. I asked the driver to drop me off at the bus station. I had decided that I would catch a bus to the ferry that crosses the My Cong River at the village of Hoa Hung.

When I arrived at the ferry, I stopped at a small sandwich shop to eat and wait for a ride.

I had thought that catching a ride would be easy since all the traffic to Vinh Long and Can Tho emerged at the ferry landing. It was sunset and I was still waiting for a military vehicle to come. Finally, I gave up and decided to ask for a ride from a Vietnamese truck driver sitting at a table across from me.

I had noticed earlier that he and a passenger had gotten out of a truck loaded with large bags of rice. I asked him in Vietnamese if he was going to Vinh Long. An advisory unit, MACV team 66, had a base at the edge of the city. I had stayed at the base on past trips through the area. He told me that I could ride with them, but I would have to ride in the back on top of the rice bags.

I agreed and walked behind the truck as he drove the vehicle onto the ferry. The ferry was about one hundred feet in length and forty feet in width. It was divided into two sections in which vehicles were parked. After the truck boarded the ferry, I stopped beside the truck bed and changed from my jungle fatigues into civilian clothes I had in a small bag. After I changed clothes, I climbed on top of the rice bags. I move a few rice bags located in the front next to the cab creating a small bunker to lay in. I hid my M-16, the bag with my fatigues, and my pistol belt in the space, climbed in and lay down out of site. I knew that ARVN Reserves had ID checkpoints along the road to Vinh Long. I figured that if I stayed out of sight, lying behind the rice bags, no one would notice me. We had traveled about halfway to Vinh Long before a checkpoint stopped us. I lay still on top of the bags and listened.

Whoever had stopped the truck jumped up on the truck running board and asked the driver what was on the back truck. The driver informed the individual that he was carrying a load of rice. The individual standing on the truck running board spoke to someone on the ground and told them to unload two bags of rice. By this time, I was becoming suspicious that they were a squad of Viet Cong troops.

I moved the M-16 into a position that made it easier to handle in case I needed to fire the weapon. I heard someone moving around at the back of the truck. Shortly after that, I heard the running board squeak as the individual standing on it changed position. I pulled the M-16 into a position that could be fired, anticipating the individual looking into the rear of the vehicle. I was greatly relieved when I heard the boots hit the pavement. After a few minutes the truck started back up and moved on down the road. Before we arrived in Vinh Long, the vehicle stopped a few hundred yards from the MACV compound.

The driver got out of the cab and came to the rear of the truck to check his load. He informed me that I did the right thing by being quiet and lying still. He told me that the individuals that stopped the truck were Viet Cong looking for food. They wanted bags of rice. He said that the incidents happen very often and that it was a cost of traveling the highways after dark. I gathered my equipment and entered the MACV compound.

I asked a Staff Sergeant on duty if I could stay the night and told him about the incident. He told me that I was lucky to have not been captured or killed. I told him that I had a praying mother and this, showing him the charming necklace. He told me that I was fortunate to have God and Budda both on my side. The Staff Sergeant told me that even MACV team members never travel alone on the highways of Vietnam. Especially through the area from the ferry to Vinh Long.

The next morning, I caught a ride with two MACV team members to Binh Thuy. After I arrived waited until the afternoon and caught a ride onto Thot Not on the chow ration truck. The company made a ration run to Binh Thuy each day. When I reached Camp Thot Not, I found the lieutenant in charge of the site and reported for duty. He informed me that early morning, Thui had come to the front gate looking for me. She had found a house directly across from the compound. Camp Thot Not was another site originally built by the Seabees to shelter the Brown Water Navy patrol boats. It was situated on the Hau River that flows from Cambodia to the gulf below Soc Trang.

The base was about five acres. The rear of the compound faced a tributary of the Hua River. The front of the compound faced QL91b, a highway that runs along the length of the river from the Can Tho to the Gulf. The highway was a two-lane road. Company B company was tasked to widen the road. This feat was accomplished by digging a ditch six feet deep and 12 feet across on each side of the road. The ditch was constructed in sections. The rice paddy was excavated down the clay layer. Water was then pumped from the ditch, and then the ditch was refilled with a mixture of lime, sand and clay. After construction on the road was completed, it was widened into a four-lane highway. The compound had a barbwire perimeter fence. Guard towers were placed on each corner of the perimeter.

There were two entrances, in front, through the main gate, and through the rear. The compound was in the center of a small village. There was a small lane that ran along the riverbank. Homes, shops and small restaurants were built along the bank. Many buildings were built on wooden pilings, with the rear of the buildings reaching out over the river. Sleeping areas were constructed with thirty-foot by twenty-foot canvas tents. Placed on wooden plank floors. The orderly room and the CO's office were situated in the center of the compound.

The house that Thui had found was seventy-five yards from the front gate. She had already purchased household cooking items and bedding. We had a small refrigerator and a propane stove. We were set up to live comfortably. We settled into our new home, and I was scheduled to start work on Monday. On the weekend before I started, we took a bus to Long Xuyen, the nearest city. Long Xuyen is in the middle of rice country. The Hua River flows through the city. The banks alongside the river are filled with shops built on piers and floating boats. In many places, boards were placed between each boat to create a walkway.

Roads and canals connected the jasmine rice farms and other small villages. The canals branched from the Hou River and ran through the countryside. The city is 45 kilometers from the Cambodian border. The area was the staging point for excursions into Cambodia by the Special Forces in 1970 and 1971. We returned home around 1700 hours on Saturday evening. It was the first peaceful weekend we had together since we got married. We were happy to find a place close to the compound so that I could go home every evening as I would on any other job.

Monday morning, I was on the compound before 0530 hours. I went to the mess hall and had breakfast. The project lieutenant came in and sat at the table with me. I had worked for him for the past eight months. We had hired Vietnamese to work in the kitchen and the mess hall dining area. It reminded me of the first few days I arrived in Vietnam; I had sat at a Mess Hall table listening to the Vietnamese language. The difference this time was I understood every word they were speaking.

"What are they talking about?" The lieutenant inquired

"Are you sure that you want to know?" I asked.

"It's frustrating to listen to someone carrying on a conversation and not understanding what is being sad," he complained.

"Well, the cute one was telling the other girl that you were handsome and that she wanted to come in early tomorrow and crawl in bed with you," I told him.

"You're joking, aren't you?" he asked.

"No sir, I am not; get ready for her to try to crawl in bed with you tomorrow," I told him.

"Well, I'll have a hard time sleeping tonight," he complained.

"If you get that hard, use your hand," I jokingly told him.

"It's worked so far," he answered.

"I'll call her over here to clean the table; say something in Vietnamese to her," he instructed me.

"Call her over," I answered.

"Trang, please come and clean our table," he requested, calling her to the table.

She came over and started wiping the table. Spending more time on the lieutenant's side of the table.

"Cô Trang, cô chú ý nhiều hơn đến phía sĩ trung úy của bàn.(Ms. Trang, you are paying more attention to the lieutenant's side of the table," I complained.

"Ồ! Bạn làm tôi ngạc nhiên khi biết bạn nói tiếng Việt"(Oh! you surprise me you speak Vietnamese), she exclaimed.

"Vâng đúng rồi, tôi có thể đọc, viết và nói tiếng Việt,"(Yes that's right, I can read write and speak Vietnamese),"I answered to her comment.

"Ai đã dạy bạn nói tiếng Việt lưu loát?" (Who taught you to speak fluent Vietnamese) she inquired.

"Vợ Việt Nam của tôi là anh chị em đã dạy tôi nói. Tôi học đọc và viết từ sách ngôn ngữ,"(My Vietnamese wife siblings taught me to speak. I learn to read and write from language books,"I answered her.

"Trung úy này nghĩ rằng bạn xinh đẹp, anh ta muốn được tha bổng cùng bạn". (This lieutenant thinks you are beautiful he wants to be acquitted with you). I told her.

"You Beautiful man too," she told the Lieutenant, turned and walked away.

"What did you say to her?" he inquired of me.

"I told her that you think she is beautiful," I told him.

"You trying to be a matchmaker," he asked with a laugh.

"Are you looking for a Vietnamese wife? I did not know of an officer who is married to a Vietnamese, but there must be one somewhere," I stated.

After we left the Mess Hall, I went to the motor pool and checked out a Duce-and-half. I would use the vehicle to transport the Vietnamese workers to the job site. The workers were used to shovel soil from sections of the ditch where the excavator arm could not reach. They also filled sandbags and placed the bags on sections of the ditch where water leaked in out of the rice fields. The work was hot and tiring; I had them stop working every hour and, take a ten-minute break and drink plenty of water. Workers with higher skill levels manned the water pumps and operated heavy equipment; nearly all were women. Early in the war, RMK-BRJ Construction discovered that women made the best heavy equipment operators. I could never understand why unless it was because women did most of the work around the home and out in the fields. The war may have turned out differently if women had been in charge. We had a crew of six operators that operated the M290 Earthmovers.

The Earthmovers were used to remove soil on the south side of the road to fill the ditch. The original road acted as a barrier separating the south side of the road. The barrier stopped water from seeping through, leaving the south side of the road dry. After a rainstorm, it was a different matter; the cut became so muddy that the equipment could not operate in the cut. Work stopped each day at noon to let the women eat lunch. They left the engines running because some of the equipment was hard to start once the engine was shut down.

The 290 operators discovered that the eight-foot-high tires on the equipment made great sunscreens. The operators and some of the unskilled workers would take their lunch break in the shade of the huge tires. They sat on the ground with their backs leaning against the treads and went to sleep after eating lunch. I had always cautioned the operators to walk around the machine to check for people who were asleep. I was on the job for a couple of weeks when an accident happened.

One of the drivers took her lunch break sitting in the cab of the tractor. After lunch, I walked over to the equipment to get everyone back to work. I saw a woman sitting on the ground behind the rear wheel of the 290M Scraper. The operator, sitting at the steering wheel, put the tractor in reverse gear and started slowly backing up.

I was shocked to see the rear wheel of the scraper slowly rolling over the woman leaning asleep against the wheel. She was pinned in a sitting position between the tire and the ground. The rolling tire bent her body forward until her head hit her knees. I started yelling and waving my arms as I ran towards the back of the scraper. The scraper kept rolling backwards until the tire was sitting on top of her body.

Her blouse bloomed outwards until it burst, spraying blood and gut all over the place. I became sick and leaned over with my head down and my hands on my knees and started heaving. The operator figured something was wrong and shut off the engine, leaving the scraper wheel setting on top of the dead woman.

I walked over to the Duce-and-half and called the lieutenant on the field radio. I stopped the work, had the crew load back onto the truck and drove them back to the compound. After we returned everyone unloaded and sat on the ground. I went into the orderly room to report to the Lieutenant and explained how the accident happened. He had me sit at his desk and write a full report of the accident. After I completed the report, I went back out to where the crew was waiting to bring the operator in and write her statement. I looked around and could not find her, one of the crew members told me that she left in a hurry. The work on the project stopped until the rest of Company B came to the base the following week.

I continued to supervise the work crew on the job site. However, things were done differently; all work crew members had lunch together, and everyone returned to work at the same time. All equipment was shut down during lunch. The White Mice (Vietnamese Police) found the operator that caused the accident. She claimed that the equipment malfunctioned, she claimed that she had shifted the gear shift to forward position, but the tractor went backwards instead of forwards. Mechanics inspected the equipment and determined that there was no malfunction in the shifting mechanism. She was fired from the work site, and the US government paid the family of the dead woman.

The routine around the compound returned to normal. I worked from 0600 to 1700 hours Monday through Friday, with most Saturdays and Sundays off. Ben Tri compound was evacuated, and all of Company B was on the Thot Not compound, including the First Sergeant and the CO. Thui always came to the compound when I returned from work in the evenings. The accident with the 290M scraper had made her uneasy when I was away. I reassured her that strict safety majors were in place to help prevent such accidents.

One afternoon, the First Sergeant approached her and asked her if she could sew. She told him that she sewed but did not have a sewing machine. He told her that he would find a sewing machine on Binh Thuy's base and bring it back to the compound. He told her that she could set up a sewing shop in one of the base's tents near the front gate. She could charge to sew on unit patches and mend fatigues. She asked him to bring a list of the prices charged on Binh Thuy, and she would do the same work for fifty percent less.

A few days later, he brought back a foot pedal sewing machine. Thui was happy with it. The machine was a Singer that one of the Supply Sergeants had in his inventory. I was surprised that he still had the machine in his inventory. A pedal Singer sewing machine brought big money in Vietnam. Such a sewing machine would allow a

Vietnamese to open a small sewing business. There was a line waiting as soon as Thui set up the business. She sewed every day while I was away on the job site.

I never knew how much money she made from the business. I would notice new civilian clothes the size to fit Americans hanging on racks inside the tent. No one stole from her, and everyone respected her by calling her Mrs. Gray. Often, in the evenings, we would walk down a lane beside the base to one of the Noodle shops along the river. The shops had the best Pho and noodle soup that I ever had while in Vietnam. The noodles were large and plump, sitting in a beef broth, and all kinds of green vegetables were piled on top. Thui always inspected the vegetables to make sure they did not contain any of the taboo vegetables restricted to us. We spent many pleasant, peaceful evenings together sitting at a table in the restaurants.

It was always peaceful and pleasant sitting with Thui at a table with the cool breeze blowing from the river. One Saturday afternoon, the day became unpleasant. A child playing down at the water's edge by the pier ran over to our table and told me that a body was floating in the water. I left Thui at the table and went to investigate. Sure enough, there was a bloated body floating in the water. The body would bump up against the side of the pier every time a small wave came in. The body seemed to be the size of an American. It was hard to tell since it was bloated and discolored, and fish had eaten at it. I ran back to the table and told Thui about the body. We walked back to the compound through the base rear entrance. I went to the orderly room and reported what the child had discovered to the First Sergeant. He told me to go to the medical tent and take the medic to where we found the body. I went and informed the medic what I had discovered.

We both mounted a M880 pickup truck that was parked in front of the orderly room. I drove through the back entrance of the compound and parked as close as possible to the body. We dismounted and walked down the riverbank to the body. The medic told me that it sure did look like an American and that we had to recover the body. The smell was horrible. I tried breathing through my mouth to prevent throwing up. I had smelled dead fish before on riverbanks when fishing back in Arkansas. However, this was the most horrible stench I had ever smelled. We went back to the compound and found a poncho to wrap around the body. I also told a couple of troops standing in front of the orderly room to climb aboard that we had a fast job to do for the First Sergeant.

I was not going to tell them that we had to go pick up a body. I was glad that Thui went back home after we returned to the base. I did not want her to tag along and see the body. We returned to where the body was in the water. We used bamboo poles to try shoving the body into a position to be wrapped in the poncho. It proved to be difficult because the body would not sink and was coming apart. The two troops I had brought along were not helpful. They refused to get near the body nor touch it with the bamboo poles. We managed to place the body on top of the poncho by tying rocks to the corners and pushing it under the body. We tied lines around the rocks to use to draw the poncho together, making a sling for the body. We pulled the body from the water onto the bank. I demanded the two troops that were with us to grab a corner and help lift the body into the bed of the M880.

The troops took off once the body was on the bed of the pickup. We drove the body to the mortuary in Binh Thuy and turned it over to Army Mortuary Affairs. The experience was more traumatic than the woman being run over by the 290M. I imagine it was because he was an American soldier. The body leaked fluids onto the bed of the M880. We never got rid of the smell. We washed the bed of the pickup with bleach gasoline, rubbed it with lime and even repainted the truck. After a few weeks, the smell always seeped through again. I refused to ride in the truck after that.

At times, I understood why troops used drugs and alcohol. The effect of the substances lessened the loneliness and anxiety of fighting in Vietnam. I overlooked troops smoking pot if they were not on duty. During my first tour in Vietnam, I witnessed accidents with weapons and vehicles involving the use of drugs. Thot Not village was located twenty-seven miles from the Cambodian border. Opium and heroin were plentiful and easy to purchase. The troops could easily find the drugs.

Often, Vietnamese civilians and/or soldiers would show up on a job site selling sex and drugs. They would walk up to a troop and ask, GI, you want happy smoke, you want boom-boom, you buy thuốc phiện? Not only could troops find drugs through the black-market hard drugs, but the American medical corps contributed to substance abuse in Vietnam during the war. Military doctors heavily prescribed speed, steroids, and painkiller pills to help improve soldiers' performance.

Company B cooks liked their pot. They were always high on pot; they smoked it and/or baked it in brownies. I never touched the brownies when they told me you might not want to try that dessert. The use of opium and heroin-laced cigarettes was also concealed. A troop could smoke them out in the open without being discovered. A carton of marijuana cigarettes or a vile of heroin, the size of a thumb, could be purchased for a Ten-dollar MPC note. I caught a troop purchasing a vial of heroin from a local while on the jobsite. I reported the purchase to the First Sergeant when I brought the crew back to the barracks after work. Later that evening, the Frist Sargent and Co went to his tent to search for drugs.

He was already under the influence of heroin when they entered his tent. The First Sergeant locked him in a metal Conex for two days. The first sergeant had our welder cut window holes and weld bars over them on the sides of the container. He then painted "**Company B Jail**" in white over the door. He said he locked the troop inside the Conex to be a deterrent to others from using drugs. Word got back to 93rd

Headquarters, and the Colonel made him remove the metal container. The First Sergeant learned fast that a soldier could not be imprisoned with a court marshal. He also discovered that the military police were the only units that could have a jail.

Company B was also doing construction on a bridge spanning over one of the Hau River tributaries near Long Xuyen. The M123A1C Prime Mover with an attached lowboy trailer was the workhorse of the engineers in Vietnam. The vehicles hauled anything that needed transporting. Company B had four of these trucks in use to haul prefabricated concrete sections to the Long Xuyen Bridge construction site. The driver of one the Tractors that I mentioned earlier in the book had named his rig 'Widow Maker'. He was using the vehicle to haul building materials to the job site. The route he was using crossed a few of the canals that were built for light vehicles and farm equipment.

The tonnage of the bridges ranged from Ten to Twelve tons. The M123A1C Tractor with a lowboy trailer weighs approximately Twenty-three tons. He had made the run on the same route for a couple of weeks. During his last run, the trailer was loaded with 8-inch by 24 feet cast-iron pipes. The weight of the vehicle loaded with the pipes was over Thirty tons. He crossed over a ten-ton weight capacity bridge, and his Tractor crashed through into the channel.

The rear wheels of the trailer stuck on the road edge of the bridge. The trailer was tilting downward, still attached to the tractor at a forty-five-degree angle. The pipes were chained together, laying on the bed of the lowboy with brackets on the side. The pipes slid over the Tractor cab, pinning the driver beneath the load. He was trapped and could not escape from under the pipes. We had to bring a crane to the accident site to remove pipes to recover the body. The soldier was married with two children.

Work had become routine for me as I went with the work crew to the job site each day. Since the entire company was at Camp Thot Not, we had plenty of help. I no longer had to drive the Duce-and-half truck. Thui was still running her on post sewing business. Life was good. I would sometimes stay after everyone left and ride to the site on the noon lunch truck or ride with the Front-end Loader. There is only one seat on Case Front-end Loader, and that is where the operator sits. One day, I decided to catch a rider on the loader. I was sitting astride the cab behind the operator.

We were halfway to the job site when the Front-end Loader engine stopped, and the operator could not steer the vehicle. It is impossible to steer a front-end load without power steering. The road we were traveling on had an unfilled 12-foot wide 8 feet deep ditch. The front-end loader wheels went off the road and catered into the ditch. As the vehicle went into the ditch, I jumped from where I was sitting behind the driver, trying to clear the vehicle in case it turned over. I jumped to the left side of the vehicle, trying to land back on the road. From where I was sitting, I was eight or nine feet high from the ground. I cleared the vehicle except for the left rear wheel. The tread caught my right arm below the shoulder and spanned both bones. When I was spun around, the tread also hit my lower back and the back of my head.

I was unconscious when I hit the ground. The front-end loader stopped without turning over. The driver jumped off and saw me lying on the ground. Blood was coming from my mouth after I bit my tongue during the fall. The driver thought I was dead, so he took off from away from the accident back towards the company to get help. I came back to consciousness after a minute or two. I lay on the ground, still in shock, with my entire body aching. I tried to rise off the ground but stopped when I felt severe pain in my right arm. I set up holding my right arm in place with my left. After a few more minutes, two soldiers jumped from the road down into the ditch. They had MACV patches on their uniforms. One of them came up to me and asked if I was ok.

I told him that I thought my arm was broken. He took a bandage rapping from a pouch on his belt and wrapped it around my arm and chest, holding my arm in place. They helped me up and tried to think of how they would get me out of the ditch. I told them to see if the front-end loader would start back up. One of them climbed in the seat, turned the engine over the vehicle started. He did not know how to operate the bucket. I gave him instructions on how to raise and lower the bucket. He lowered the bucket to the ground, I stepped on it, and he lifted the bucket up until it was high enough for me to step off onto the road. He did the same for his partner, Then lowered it halfway, climbed on top and jumped out of the ditch. They drove the thirty-minute drive to the hospital at Binh Thuy. The doctors x-rayed my arm and told me that it was broken in three places between my shoulder and my elbow. I was feeling very good thirty minutes later after they shot me up with morphine. I was assigned to a hospital after they placed a cast on my arm. The cast covered the top portion of my body, leaving only my left arm and head exposed.

I awoke the next morning when they were bringing us patients for our morning breakfast. After breakfast, the ward was visited by a Full Bird Colonel. He was handing out Purple Hearts to troops wounded in action. He stopped by my bed and asked what had happened to me. I explained how I had received my injury. He asked me if there were any Viet Cong in the area. I told him I was sure there were but that I had not seen any. He said that it was too bad, that I could have received a Purple Heart also. I told him to save them for the guys that were being shot at. He laughed and said he thought the same, that it was one medal he did not want to earn.

Later that afternoon, the First Sergeant brought Thui to the hospital. He told me that she was shaken up after the loader operator came back and reported the accident. She had ridden to the site of the accident with the medic and the first sergeant. After arriving at the accident site and not seeing me around, they deduced that someone had stopped and rendered aid. The first sergeant used the field radio to call Binh Thuy Hospital.

The hospital informed him I was ok and that I was admitted with a broken arm. I rode with Thui and the first sergeant back to camp Thot Not. I laid around the house for a few days, recuperating from my injury. After a week, I went back and reported it to the first sergeant, telling him that I was ready to go back to work. He told me to wait around and that he would think about a job for me. After discussing the matter with the CO, he came back and asked if I still had my Forty-five.

After I assured him that I did, he told me to go to the front gate and wait for him. I went back home and, retrieved my 45, and walked back to the front gate carrying the weapon in my left hand. He told me that he should send me back stateside, but my language skills were invaluable. We had lost our Vietnamese interpreter to 93rd headquarters after the battalion commander discovered that I was fluent in Vietnamese. The first sergeant gave me the job of guarding the front gate from 0600 hours until 1700 hours. I could only hold the weapon in my right hand. The first sergeant came when I went on duty and injected a round in the chamber, and cleared the weapon after duty. This was my daily routine for the next eight weeks.

****

Chapter 12

Company B completed most of the Can Tho to Long Xuyen Road project around May 1971. Our next project was to continue widening the road west of Long Xuyen to Chao Duc. Chau Doc is in the northwest corner of the Mekong Delta. The city is approximately 3 miles from the Cambodian border. The city lies between the Hau Giang River and a made Canal. Chau Doc base was on the Bassac River, another Brown Water navy base used to support the River Patrol boats. The base was located where the Bassac River and a canal reached a point.

The base area covered approximately five square acres. I was much the same size as Thot Not Base. However, I was located about five miles from the QL 91, our job site. A channel ran along the base on the north side. An ARVN compound was adjacent to the base on the west side. The east and south sides were surrounded by rice paddies butting against the jungle. I went with the advance troops to help hire workers and security guards.

By 1971, most bases used Vietnamese nationals to provide base perimeter security, and I oversaw the security force and restrictions on access to the compound through the front gate entrance. A five-mile gravel road ran from the compound out to QL 91. The entire area had become a small village with rice fields and bamboo thatch roof huts hastily constructed alongside the gravel road. Most of the huts were occupied by family members of ARVN soldiers stationed on the adjacent compound. Thui came with me when I left Thot Not with the advanced party.

She found us a place to stay in one of the bamboo huts about one hundred yards from the front gate. She negotiated a rent price that included furniture and a stove. The hut did not have a refrigerator, so we kept blocks of ice in Styrofoam coolers to keep drinks and perishable foods cold. There was no electricity in the area, and Coleman-type lanterns provided all lighting. At times, the hut reminded me of the sharecropper farmhouse I lived in as a child. The house was for farmhands that worked on my grandmother's farm. Every time it rained, we had to set pots and pans under the leaks through the roof to keep the floor dry. The hut had a hard-packed clay floor. When we arrived at the base, it was empty, except for tons of fifty-five-gallon fuel and oil drums. All wooden structures had been demolished and taken away by the Vietnamese. We had to build a berm around the compound on the three sides facing away from the river. We hauled in eight-foot pipe culverts and placed them around the perimeter. We then covered the ends and fronts with plywood sheets. We covered the ends and tops with dirt and sand we dredged from the river. In the center of the compound, we built an orderly room, wooden barracks, a mess hall dining facility and a company club. The motor pool was situated to the rear next to the river. It took us three weeks to rebuild the compound.

The rest of Company B arrived after we constructed the compound. Soon, everything became routine again. I manned the gate during the day and made security checks twice each night. We were lucky to find a place close to the front gate. It was easy for me to get up and do my security checks during the night. I always carried a flashlight with a red lens to signal the guard at the gate tower that I was coming in. I dared not approach the gate unless I received a return signal. Most of the time, the guards were jumpy and would fire at anything that moved outside of the perimeter. One night around midnight, I was making my rounds around the perimeter, checking the guards up in the towers.

I was sitting in a corner tower on the compound's east side, talking to a guard. My seat was at the M60 machine gun firing position. The guard called my attention to a shadow next to the barbed wire at the edge of the perimeter. The shadow was crawling through the barbed wire, moving towards the inside.

When I called out for the shadow halt, it jumped up and scrambled through the wire into the compound and disappeared. I took out my 45, injected a round in the chamber and climbed back down the ladder; I hurried and woke the CO and First Sergeant and reported that we may have had a sapper come inside the compound. He told me to get a squad together and search for the sapper inside the compound. Searching the compound for the individual was nerve-racking.

We had over 100 fifty-five-gallon oil drums scattered throughout the area around the motor pool. Some were lying on the side, and some were standing. All the containers had the lids removed. I cautiously walked through the drum storage, shining my light around and inside the drums. I kicked a drum if the tops were sitting on the ground, fearing that the individual had slipped a drum over their head. It took the rest of the night to check the compound. I did find tracks leading from the perimeter to inside the compound. However, we did not find anyone on the compound that did not belong there. It seemed the sapper had egressed the base as easily as they had entered.

About three days after the perimeter breach, we detained a Vietnamese man who sneaked in on base. He was discovered near the area where building supplies were kept. The troops apprehended and brought him to the front gate so I could interrogate him. He did not have a Vietnamese national ID card, nor would he tell his name or where he lived. After he was apprehended, the troops tied his hands behind his back and placed a rope around his neck.

After questioning him for ten minutes and not getting any information, I decided to try another tactic. I turned over a trash can sitting beside my desk and had the two troops pick him up and stand him on top. I threw the end of the rope over a rafter and tied it tight enough that he had to stand on his toes. I started questioning him again. Every time he did not answer, I would kick the trash can. He started crying and praying to Budda after I kicked the can three or four times. He began begging me not to hang him and that he had a wife and children that depended on him. Feeling sorry for him, I loosened the rope from the rafter and had him sit down on the upside-down trash can.

Further questioning revealed there was a hole in the fence on the ARVN side of the base he entered through and stole things since our arrival. We placed him in the back of a jeep and transported him to a local police station. I am sure that the White Mice released him because I saw him standing in front of a bar the troops frequented. We also patched the area of the fence where he entered by moving the Jail Conex in front of the hole. It was good thinking by the first sergeant that the next time he was caught, we would lock him in it and feed him bread and water.

On an afternoon about three months later, our commo operator came up to me and informed me that I was to be at the CID office in Binh Thuy the following morning. It was the first time I had really become frightened since I had come to Vietnam. I knew that the CID would not want to be questioning me unless it was pertaining to black market activities. I went home and informed Thui about my summons to the CID office. She also became frightened and started crying. She begged me not to tell the CID about her father's involvement in the matter.

I promised her that she would not worry that I had a story made up for any questions. The next morning, I informed the first sergeant about the message the commo sergeant had received from Binh Thuy CID office. He told me to take his jeep and go find what they wanted.

I arrived at the Binh Thuy CID office just before lunch. The office was in a long mobile trailer located near the entrance of the base. I entered the office and informed an individual dressed in civilian clothes that I had been summoned to the office. The first thing he asked was, where was where is your escort? I told him that I did not have an escort, that I had come of my own accord. He led me to a desk near the rear of the office.

Another Investigator introduced himself to me and asked if I knew why I was called to the CID field office. I informed him that I didn't have any idea. He asked me if I knew anyone from the 65th Transportation stationed at Dong Tam. My heart almost failed me when he asked the question. At once, I knew the reason for my summons to the office and was thankful I already had a story prepared.

"I don't really know anyone in that company. I have played cards a few times with some of the truck drivers."I replied to the question.

"Did one of the drivers sell you a Five-ton Dump truck? " he inquired.

"No one sold me anything. However, one evening after a game of cards, one of the drivers approached me outside the hooch and asked me if I knew how he could sell a dump truck," I replied.

"Did you find a buyer for him?" he inquired further.

"I did introduce him to an ARVN captain who wanted a dump truck," I answered in reply.

"How did you arrange the sale?" he inquired again.

"I did not arrange a sell; I just introduced him to the ARVN captain," I answered.

"What was the ARVN captain's name, and what unit is he in?". He again asked.

"Sir, I know where the unit is located and the captain's name; I don't know the name of the unit," I replied.

"What is the captain's name? Could you take us to the ARVN compound? He requested.

"His name is Đại úy Trường, and the compound is located on highway QL1 between My Tho and Long An," the name I made up, and the location was an ARVN compound I remembered once passing.

"We need you to go with us to the compound and show us the ARVN officer. Did you receive any money making the deal?" he inquired.

"No, I did not receive any money; however, he promised to give me an NVA ARK 54 pistol when he came across one. So far, I have not heard from him since I introduced him to the driver."I replied.

We left the compound in a military police jeep and made the trip south across the ferry on down to the ARVN compound. We turned off the highway and drove down a dirt road to the compound. I introduced myself as the ARVN soldier standing guard at the base entrance.

"Tôi là Trung sĩ Gray, bạn của Đại úy Trường Chúng tôi có hẹn với anh ấy,"(I am Sergeant Gray a friend of Captain Truong, we have an appointment with him) I announce to the guard.

"Không có sĩ quan nào ở đây có tên đó,"(There is no officer here by that name). We were informed.

"Tôi yêu cầu bạn yêu cầu chỉ huy đại đội đến nói chuyện với chúng tôi."(I demand you ask the company commander to come and talk to us.) I requested the agent to sit in the passenger's seat. I had no knowledge that he spoke Vietnamese. After a few minutes, an ARVN Captain came to the gate. The CID agent who spoke Vietnamese tried his best to get Captain Truong's attention. He finally gave up and told us that the ARVN Officer had probably lied about his name and unit. He said that was also the reason I did not hear from him again. It made sense to me since I had made up the entire scenario. On our way back to Binh Thuy, the CID agent asked if I wanted to know how they discovered who the driver who stole the Five-Ton dump truck was. I told him that it must be an interesting story.

He told me that they searched all the troop's bunks in the 65th Transportation Company. During the search, he found Five Hundred dollars in MPC notes stashed under the mattress of one of the truck drivers. After an interrogation, the driver told him that he sold the truck to me for five hundred dollars. The agent said he was more inclined to believe my account of the transaction. He said I had more credibility since I was upfront from the beginning and did not deny I knew about the driver making the deal.

We arrived at Binh Thuy around 1500 hours. It was too late to make the drive back to Chau Doc. I went to 93rd Headquarters, checked in and bunked out in a transit hooch. The next morning, I was approached by the Sergeant Major, who informed me that the battalion commander wanted to see me in his office before I left for Chau Doc. I walked with the sergeant major over to the Battalion headquarters office. The Sergeant Major stepped into the Colornal's office, then after a few minutes, came back and out. He told me to go on in and don't forget to report. I went into the colonel's office, stood in front of his desk, saluted smartly, and reported to him. He was much nicer than I had imagined him to be. He questioned me about the incident involving the CID office. I told him everything that I knew. When I was through, he looked at me and shook his head.

"I don't know if I should Court Marshall you or give you a medal," he told me.

"Sir, I don't want either. I know now I should have at least reported the conversation I had with the truck driver to his first sergeant. If I had, he might not be in as much trouble as he is now." I told the Colonel.

"Well, I hope you learned a lesson from the incident. You are dismissed to return to your company. Keep doing the good job that I have heard about." he said as he turned back to his desk and started shuffling through papers lying on top of his desk.

"Thank you, sir," I said as I did an about-face and left the office.

It was around noon when I returned to Chau Dok. Thui was sitting in front of the hut, so I stopped and told her that everything was alright, that there was nothing to worry about, I had straightened everything out. She told me that she was sick from worry and had not slept since I had left. I told her that I had to go on to the base and report to the First Sargeant that I would come back home later.

Later in the week, one evening around 2000 hours, a troop came running to find me. He told me that the White Mice had raided the huts in the area where Thui and I lived. He informed me that a group of about twenty women were apprehended and loaded onto the rear of a Duce-and-Half. I ran back to the front gate and saw the vehicle driving away.

Thui was sitting in the rear of the vehicle on the right side next to the tailgate. I ran back to where the Jeeps were parked, jumped in, and started it up. I sped through the front gate and raced down the road to catch the disappearing vehicle. I finally caught up with the vehicle as it was pulling into the Chau Doc police station. The vehicle had stopped, and the women aboard were being unloaded. They were being marched single file into a containment room. I followed them inside and confronted the White Mouse guarding the women.

"Officer, you have my wife in the group of women you just brought in," I informed him in Vietnamese.

"Which one is your wife?" he inquired.

"Ms Vo Thi Thui as indicated on her national ID card. That's her over there. I told him, indicating where Thui was standing, separated from the rest of the group.

"All those women were in an area that is off limits as ordered by Captain Chang," he informed me.

"Who is Captain Chang?" I inquired, beginning to become angry.

"Captain Chang is the base commander of the ARVN base in the area."

"I want to talk to your commander now," I insisted.

"He went home to his family. He will not return until tomorrow morning; your wife will have to stay here until tomorrow morning," he told me.

"She will be released to me at once. We are legally married by both American and Vietnamese law. If she is not released at this moment, I will go out to my jeep and call her uncle. Her uncle is Major General Van Mung Duong. He would be very unhappy to hear that you abducted his niece," I threaten.

It was a bluff, and I did not know Major General Van Mung Dung. I remembered the name from a Vietnamese TV news report. The bluff worked because he immediately went and brought Thui over to me. He apologized and rubbed his hands to gather as if praying to Buddha. I noticed among the huddled women the Mama san that owned the bar frequented by most of the company. There were also a couple of girls standing beside her that she employed. I called the three women over to where I was standing and asked if they had their national ID cards. She told me that the White Mice had confiscated everyone's ID cards. I order the police officer to return the ID cards to the three women. Thui had her ID card because she refused to give it up when she was apprehended. I told the officer that the three women worked on base and that I was also taking them with me. He didn't argue with me; he was glad to be rid of me and Thui.

It was nearly midnight when we returned to the Compound. I dropped Thui and the other women off at our home, then entered the compound and parked the jeep. I still had my security rounds to complete, so I walked the perimeter, checking on the guards. I stopped at the tower in the corner that overlooked the front side of the base and the ARVN compound. The guard had watched the White Mice raid on the village. He told me that the raid occurred because the ARVN captain of the base was jealous of the Americans who frequented the club. The hookers in the club would not do business with the Vietnamese troops.

The ARVN commander asked one of his White Mice buddies to raid the village in front of the compound. They were to round up all the younger women living in the area and carry them to Police headquarters. Thui was unfortunate that she had been caught in the raid. She had shown the police her National ID card and her marriage license. Luckily, her mother kept her passport and visa in a lock box at home, or she may have lost them.

While I was sitting in the tower talking to the guard, I noticed two GIs standing near the fence separating the base from the ARVN compound. One of them was holding something, a round object in his hand. He pointed it at the ARVN compound, and a flare shot from it and went through the entrance of one of the buildings. Soon after, ARVN troops fled the building naked or half-dressed. I recognized the individual when the light from the flare lit his face. I wish that I had been looking the other way because later, I had to identify him. He had done something that any of us wish we had done first. We learned the next day that the flare had given two of the ARVN troops third-degree burns. Our CO ordered his executive officer to investigate the incident. Since I witnessed the incident, I had to write a full report naming the two individuals standing at the fence and identifying the one who shot the flare.

One of the women that I rescued from Chau Doc jail was the girlfriend of our supply sergeant. She had stayed the night with Thui after we returned to the base. She was afraid of reprisals from the White Mice still hanging around the village. She felt safe under the protection of Thui and me. Thui became a celebrity when it was discovered that she was the niece of a (Make-believe) Vietnamese Major General. Officers in the ARVN compound also learned of the relationship through the White Mice grapevine. Thui also enjoyed newfound respect from all the women in the small village. The next day, the supply sergeant came to me and inquired about the White Mice raid on the village the evening before.

After I explained to him what had happened, he was concerned about his girlfriend. She was in love with him and determined to marry him. She was further encouraged by the example of Thui and me and believed that she could have the same happiness.

The supply sergeant knew that there was no way he could talk her into going back to her parents. It was the same story around every base in Vietnam. In 1971 and 72, about 900 Vietnamese and American marriages occurred, and only 279 were service members. By the middle of 1971, the statistics had tripled. American embassy officials believe the increase was due to a rapid reduction in the American military throughout Vietnam. Soldiers hurriedly married for fear of being sent home and becoming permanently separate from Vietnamese girlfriends. This was my greatest fear until Thui and I landed at Ohara Airport in 1972. Americans walking the streets of Saigon with their Vietnamese girlfriends or wives were constantly the target of harassment from the White Mice. These police stood dressed in White uniforms (thus the nickname, White Mice) at street intersections directing traffic. They would stop taxis with American males and Vietnamese women riding together as passengers and demand National ID cards. The incident with Thui and the other women in the village was a good example of this type of harassment.

The supply sergeant and I came up with a plan for him to keep her on post without being detected by the First sergeant. The Vietnamese were not the only ones who harassed service members with Vietnamese girlfriends; top-ranked NCOs and Officers had their reasons, too. As I mentioned earlier, the perimeter around the compound was large pipe culverts with the ends covered with plywood. Dirt was dozed over the structures to create berm bunkers.

Most of the bunkers become single living quarters for ranks Staff Sargeant and above. The supply sergeant lived in one of the bunkers. The first sergeant made rounds around 1700 hours to try to catch women staying on post with their boyfriends. A staff sergeant in our company received a disciplinary article 15 and lost a grade in rank when his girlfriend was caught in his room after curfew. We devised a way that the supply sergeant would most likely not be caught with his girl in his room after curfew.

We disconnect the plywood sheeting on the rear of the culbert facing inside the berm. We mounted a rod on top and bottom and fashioned the plywood to swing open and shut. It did not show that the rear wall had become a door. We then dug a space 5 feet high, 5 feet deep and 6 feet wide; the space made a nice covey hole for hooch maid to hide in until the First sergeant made his rounds. Since I was the one who controlled the sign-in and out register, I carried the register over to the sergeant's room and had her sign out every evening. She managed to stay on the compound without leaving until we vacated the base.

****

Chapter 13

It was late in November 1971 when we turned the compound over to the ARVNs, packed everything up and relocated to Binh Thuy. We were lucky to move away from the area when we did because the base was overrun during the 1972 Easter offensive. All ARVN troops on both bases were captured or killed. When we arrived back to Binh Thuy Company B was in the area reserved for the 93rd Engineers. Since we only had three months left before Thui and I were to go to the States, Thui went back to her home in My Tho.

I stayed at Binh Thuy and helped with preparing equipment to be sent back to the states. First, we drained all the fuel from the fuel tanks on all the equipment. Next, we hooked hoses to vehicle exhaust pipes and stuck the ends inside the fuel tanks. We let the exhaust fumes pump into the tank for ten minutes to evacuate all fuel fumes from the fuel tanks. We did more maintenance preparing the vehicles for shipment back to the States than we did during the time the equipment was in Vietnam. It was the two loneliest months I spent in Vietnam.

A few days after the company arrived in Binh Thuy, I was called into the CO office. He showed me a congressional letter the Battalion had received from Illinois congressman Stevenson. The letter referred to me not contacting my parents for two years. I was ordered to go to the MARS station and wait until I contacted my parents. The MARS was the way soldiers and sailors could personally communicate with loved ones back home. The system was a short-wave radio telephone patch. MARS stations would allow a soldier a five minutes of ham radio telephone call home to the United States. The most important thing for the system to work was to say "over" each time you were through commenting. The ham radio operators had to hear the command to know when to switch microphones.

I got through to my mother over the system quickly. As soon as I contacted her, I told her to let me talk until I was through before she said anything. I told her that I was only allowed five minutes to talk and that it was difficult to use the system. I told her everything that I was just fine and had married a Vietnamese. I was bringing her home with me when we left Saigon on February 27th and landed at Ohara Airport in Chicago. I told her that I would call as soon as I reached an airport in the States. After I was through talking, I had about two minutes of airtime left. I told her that she could talk now and not stop until she was through saying everything she wanted to say. I explained it was like me reading my letter to her, and she was reading hers to me. It was the hardest two minutes of my life. The only thing that I feared about going to Vietnam was dying and breaking my mother's heart. I was so ashamed that I had broken her heart that much, even without dying.

I got my DEROS (Date Eligible for Return from Overseas) orders in the middle of December. I had 45 days of accumulated leave. I had not had annual leave since my arrival in Vietnam. All my leave was a few days in the country and squeezed in between changing duty stations. I left Company B On December 23rd and caught a lift on a Huey going to Dong Tam.

I hired a three-wheeled taxi to take me the rest of the way to Thui's home. When I arrived, she acted as if we had been apart for a year. She had not been as active as she had been. She had plenty of time to mope and worry about everything. She told me when I was not around to reassure her that her mind flew in every direction. She complimented every kind of scenario, from me being killed by a mortar round that was always being fired into Binh Thuy's base. She thought of the military sending me back to the States without giving me time to come and pick her up. One thing that I was glad about was that any of the scenarios did not involve me just up and leaving. I showed her my DEROS orders and our plane tickets. The flight time was 1000 hours on February 27th, 1972. She held the papers next to her heart as if they were precious to her. After a few minutes, she showed them to her mother, who locked the orders and tickets in her lockbox. I thought to myself. I sure hope nothing happens to that lockbox; I really needed not to worry; Mrs. Vo guarded that box with her life.

Vo was not Thui's mother's name. I refer to her as Mrs. Vo in this book because Thui's father's name was Vo van Nguyen. Thui's mother was of the Nguyen Royal bloodline.

Four names, Nguyen Nhi Thit Trang, were printed on her Vietnamese National ID card. Nguyen was her family name, Nho her given name and Thi and Trang her middle names. She was always treated with profound respect when any official read her name on her ID card. Thui's parents came from the Dai Lat, a city in the central highlands of Vietnam. Mrs. Vo often told me the story of how Thui's grandparents met. Thui's grandmother was from a wealthy family that always gave food aid to the less fortunate. Once monthly, she loaded a wagon with food and distributed the food to peasants living in the countryside.

Mr. Vo's father was a Warlord directly related to General Võ Nguyên Giáp. One month, she was captured by Thui's grandfather, and she was forced to marry him. He accomplishes this task by burying her in the sand with only her head above ground. He told her that he would leave her buried until she promised to marry. Seven days later, she gave up and made the promise.

They were married on the spot by a Buddhist monk. The Warlord's grandfather consummated the marriage and let her go. Thui's grandmother returned to the walled compound and reported the incident to her father. A price was placed on the grandfather's head.

After Thui's grandmother discovered that she was with child, she ran away and located the Warlord's grandfather. That was the beginning of Thui's family. Thui informed me that the Japanese slaughtered both grandparents.

Mrs. Vo's family trip involved the entire family, including Thui's aunt and cousin and the monk's uncle. The first stop was the city of Dalat then to the beach at Vung Tau. She hired a small bus that held all our group, including food and clothing. We followed Highway CT01 to Dalat. We drove during, between 0900 hours and 1700 hours, the safest time to travel the highways in Vietnam in 1971. We made numerous rest stops and spent the night at a hotel in one of the cities Mrs Vo had marked on her map. It took us two days to reach Dalat.

In 1955, Mr. and Mrs. Vo lived in Dalat, where they ran a small restaurant. They sold the restaurant and moved to My Tho in 1964. Thui was fifteen years old at the time. Thanh, her younger brother, was twelve. She also had a second younger brother and three sisters when the family settled at My Tho. Mrs Vo lost all the money from the sale of the restaurant when her handbag was stolen after the family reached My Tho. On the first day, we went sightseeing around the City of Dalat. Buildings in the city were mainly influenced by the French, who built most of the city during the colonial period.

The Railway Starion was built in 1938 in a style that incorporated French design with high-pointed roofs of the Cao Nguyen dynasty. The interior of the station was designed with a high arched ceiling and colored glass windows. It was one of the most beautiful buildings I have seen in Vietnam. It was an example of what Vietnam was and what it could become. We visited three mansions of the Vietnamese last Emperor Bao Dai, built by the French in 1940 and sold to Emperor Bio Dai in 1949. The mansion was as used as a summer mansion for all presidents of the Republic of Vietnam until 1975. The Second Mansion was the French Indochina governor to be used as a summer mansion. The third mansion was the residence of Emperor Bao Dai and his family.

All we did was take pictures of the mansions; they were all closed to the public, and we were not allowed to go inside. We didn't have much time to look around; it would have taken us two weeks to view all the sites. I had bought a Canon A-1 35mm Camera with a 50mm lens, at the post exchange before I left Binh Thuy. I wanted to take pictures around My Tho and other places we went before we left for the States. Thanh, Thui's brother, was our cameraman and took all the pictures of our family trip. Thanh and four other siblings of Thui immigrated to London after the fall of Saigon in 1975. He was able to take most of the pictures of our family trip with him. He and his siblings still live in London. They visited us in 1993 while I was living in Portland, Oregon.

After Dalat, we continued our trip to the beach at Vung Tau, a place where there seemed to be no war. It was the first time I had visited the city. Vung Tau was one of the best (R&R) in-country destinations for soldiers who needed some time for relaxation and recreation. The R&R spot is beautiful and has peaceful beaches to relax on, swim, or surf. It was much like Hawaii or California beaches: dotted umbrella chairs and surfboard stands that rented surfboards. Since I was from Arkansas, I had never been on an ocean beach. We camped out on Black Beach for four days.

Thanh and his siblings bought fish from local fishermen. The fishermen were sitting in houses on stilts attached to nets stretching out into the ocean. The ropes stretched between concrete pilings placed approximately fifty feet apart. Some of the nets stretched four hundred yards out into the ocean. The fishermen were walking the ropes like circus performers. They ran up and down the lines, feet on bottom ropes and hands clinging to ropes stretched overhead. They would stop between pilings and draw the nets up out of the water. As they pulled the nets up hand-over-hand, they removed fish caught in the nets.

They dropped the fish in a basket hanging by straps across their shoulders. Thui's uncle told me that the fishermen in this area had fished like this for hundreds of years. We cooked fish and lobsters that weighed at least six pounds each. They were so big I could not finish one of them. We returned to Saigon on the fifth day and toured the city the rest of the day. Late in the evening, we arrived at the aunt's home in Tan An in time for a late dinner. She cooked a big meal for us. Again, I was fortunate that I loved Nuoc Mum, rice and any other type of Vietnamese food because that was all we had during the next four days. She did not offer meat because she did not want to offend the monk. Uncle was still with us.

****

Chapter 14

Thui and I had planned to stay at her aunt's home until our departure date. I was not comfortable with my orders, tickets, passport and visa not in our procession. Neither was Thui. We decided to return to My Tho with her parents and retrieve everything that we had left at the Vo's. We would return to the aunt's home in a few days after we said goodbye to all Thui's siblings. This would be the last time I sleep on the bamboo mat with Thui's two brothers. It was much the same as the first few months that I had stayed the night with the family. I sleep with the two boys on a platform on a bamboo mat. Thui, her sisters and her mother slept together in another room. Mr. Vo became a little distant towards me; I knew that he was bothered about something. The next day, I invited him to have lunch, just us men. We went to a small restaurant that served thịt bò cuốn bánh tráng. The dish was one of my favorites, with ingredients of beef wrapped in rice paper, sprinkled with ground peanuts and dipped in Nuoc Mum sauce. As we ate, I spoke to him in Vietnamese because he could not speak much English.

"Bố (Bah) vọ.(yuar), father of wife, I have noticed that you have become saddened. You spend much time alone not talking much to me or Thui. It seems that you have become this way since we went on our family trip. I know that you are worried about Thui moving to America. We will not be away forever; I plan to return to Vietnam when I am released from the military in November of 1976. I have some friends who work for RMK-LBJ construction company. The company would hire me now if I were not a service member. Thui will be safe in America and loved by my family as much as hers loves me.

I have a large extended family. My father has four brothers and two sisters, and my mother has two sisters. All my uncles and aunts would do anything for me. I have many cousins, of which I am second from being the oldest. We will send money to you and mother when we can. I am sure that Thui can find a job if she wishes. We plan for her to go to college and earn a degree. She loves to cook; she can go to a school that teaches cooking. In America she does not entirely have to depend on me. I will give her the freedom to do anything she wants with her life. I hope that I will always be involved in it. I am leaving my Army Colt 45 with you; keep it hidden well. I may need it someday when I return to Vietnam. Again, this is one request that I later regretted making of him. I raised my shirt and held up the Tiger Tooth Charm for him to see. Ba Vo, every time I view this Tiger Tooth in a mirror or feel it with my fingers, I will remember Vietnam, you, mother and Thui's siblings. To me, living here in Vietnam was not a burden like it was to most American soldiers. I have loved every minute that I have lived here. Vietnam is like a second home; I would like someday to bring my children here to visit their grandparents," I stopped and looked at him. His mood seemed to brighten, and he was in better spirits when we went back home.

Thui and her mother had also been busy while Mr. Vo and I were at the restaurant. She had a large suitcase packed with our wedding pictures and other family pictures. All the pictures were still inside the frames. She became upset when I told her that the seashell-designed, engraved black lacquered frames had to stay.

All the frames together must have weighed at least twenty pounds. I explained that each of us was only allowed two suitcases. Each suitcase could not weigh over sixty-five pounds. She removed the pictures from the frames, wrapped them in a silk scarf and placed them in a suitcase. The suitcase also contained her wedding Ao Dias and other clothing she wished to take to America. She filled one suitcase full of Vietnamese food. It had twelve bottles of Nuoc Mun, bottles of Mum loc, sheets of rice paper, and hot Vietnamese chili peppers. We had one suitcase that was not full. I put the picture frames back into that suitcase, along with a Dan Bau, a unique traditional musical instrument that I bought for my father. The instrument makes a rustic sound by pulling a bow across the one string on the instrument. My father loves stringed instruments and asked me to bring them with me. I had enough room in the suitcase to put a lacquered jewelry cabinet for my mother, a dismantled Type-1 NVA SKS carbine that I had purchased from an ARVN soldier for fifty dollars in 1970. I was still lucky I had the weapon after all the numerous changes in duty stations.

We were packed and ready to return to the States by February the 23rd, 1972. I will always remember the day we left My Tho. Thui's mother came into the room holding the Emerald Green Jade necklace. The neckless Thui had worn on her wedding day. She placed the necklace around Thui's neck, stood back and looked her in the face.

She then said to Thui, "Dear daughter, you are my firstborn and the dearest to my heart. The necklace you have around your neck is as precious as you are. It is passed down to you through five generations. Always wear it around your neck and never take it off until you pass it on to your daughter. Thui hugged her mother and told her, Mom, don't worry, I will guard it forever. There will be times that I have to take off. When I do, it won't be for long. When it is off my neck, I will always keep it in a safe place."

We said goodbye and climbed into the Taxi we had hired to take us to Saigon. We planned to spend three days in Saigon before we boarded the plane home. We both had mixed feelings when the 27th final arrived. We loaded our suitcases into the last taxi ride we would have in Vietnam. We took the taxi to Tan Son Nhut Air Base to board a Pam Am flight to Chicago O'Hare Field. The one thing I remember while sitting in the terminal was a young Eurasian teen. She had an Army backpack slung over her shoulders and was carrying a Dàn Tranh (a plucked zither). Vietnamese traditional instruments with a long soundbox with steel strings and movable bridges. The tuning pegs or on top at the bottom of the instrument.

I walked over to her to get a good look at the instrument. I asked her about it, she told me the name of the instrument and showed me how to play it. It had a beautiful sound. After seeing the instrument, I regretted that I had not found one to take back to my dad. She told me that her American father had met her mother in Vietnam in 1954 when he went to Saigon on R&R while fighting in Korea. I felt kindness towards her, thinking someday, at eighteen years of age, she could be my daughter. After we boarded the flight, Thui sat by the window seat. She told me that she wanted to take one last look at Vietnam. Again, I had mixed feelings about leaving Vietnam. I was so happy that I was finally able to take Thui to my home country but deeply saddened that I was taking her away from hers. When the aircraft left the runway and took the air, I heard a few people cheering.

From the looks of their haircuts, I took most of them to be soldiers happy to be returning home to their families and loved ones. I looked around and noticed a few more American and Vietnamese couples sitting together. They all had sullen looks; I imagined that they were experiencing the same mixed feelings Thui and I were experiencing. After stopping for a short delay at LA airport, we boarded a Delta flight to Chicago O'Hare field.

The weather had been mild and similar when we stopped at LA airport. It was a different story when we arrived at Ohare Field. There were three feet of snow on the ground. My parents were at the airport waiting for us. My mother came running from the waiting area to meet us when we exited the passenger terminal. She ran and threw her arms around both sobbing with happiness. The first thing she said was, you both are too skinny. Later, Thui told me that she was taken aback, thinking that my mother disapproved of her because she was too skinny. My mother said that to us, and stepping outside into the freezing 10-degree weather was the beginning of a series of culture shocks that have lasted until today.

We arrived at my parents' home in Earlville, Illinois, late into the night. Thui and I were worn out from jet lag. She dozed off while sitting on the living room sofa. We had moved from the farm in Arkansas to Earlville in the Spring of 1968. My parents and my mother's younger sister had moved there to work in a factory that made electric engines.

They were living in a Double Wide Trailer in Earlville trailer park. My mother told me to wake her up and that we were to sleep in my parents' bed. She had not bought a bed for the spare room in the trailer because she wanted Thui to choose her new bed. The sofa that we were sitting on folded out into a queen-sized bed. I told my mother that I would make the bed for us to sleep on while Thui took a shower. After Thui took a shower, we both lay down and I was immediately asleep. A few years later, Thui told me what she heard my mother say to my father as they sat in chairs across the room, thinking we were asleep. My mother told my father I never would have thought he would have married someone like that. My father had told her, remember my mother did not want us to marry either. Those few words my mother said stuck with Thui until today.

****

This is the First Book of The Vietnamization of Private Gray

Three Book Sequel

First Book: Coming out, November 2024

Second Book: The Emerald Green Neckless; Coming out, July 2025

Third Book: American Gisha: Coming out, December 2025

Milton Keynes UK
Ingram Content Group UK Ltd.
UKHW051852051224
452013UK00020B/316

9 798330 588817